Praise for *Selling to the Government*

"Selling to the government is not for the faint of heart . . . you need passion for the mission, patience for the process, and the ability to persevere through administration and agency changes that happen frequently. Government is a complex marketplace, but is absolutely the most rewarding! Be a good partner to government, build solid relationships and it will pay off. In his book *Selling to the Government*, Mark Amtower provides the quintessential primer on the government marketplace. A how-to manual for those looking to enter it and a reference for seasoned professionals, it is packed with solid guidance throughout."

—Teresa H. Carlson, Vice President for the Federal
Government, Microsoft Corporation

"Mark's insights on how to penetrate the federal market show his serious knowledge of government business. Are you serious enough to follow them?"

—Larry Allen, President of The Coalition
for Government Procurement

"Many people in Washington may think they know a lot about selling to the U.S. government, but few will claim that they know more than Mark Amtower does. Mark is awesome! Mark understands the bureaucratic thought process, he understands how to communicate with these people, he knows how to get into the right door, and he is most creative when he puts it all together into a plan of action."

— Dendy Young, CEO, McLean Capital, LLC

"It's the same mistake . . . over and over. During the two decades that I have worked in public sector marketing, I have witnessed a myriad of highly successfully, commercially proven companies struggle when initially entering the government market. Why? They fail to invest the time and resources to fully understand how and why government agencies make procurement decisions.

This book from Mark Amtower is a must-read for any corporate, sales, or marketing executive interested in doing business with the U.S. federal government. Mark shares a set of best practices, lessons learned, and advice in an easy-to-read and informative writing style that will put any company on a fast path to success."

— Marc Hausman, President and CEO, Strategic
Communications Group, Inc.

"What some may fear, Mark Amtower clarifies and simplifies. The federal government has money and pays its bills on time. Read Mark's guide and "Go for it." You will have no regrets."

—Tom Carroll, Founder and Chairman, Carroll
Publishing and GovSearch

"Mark is well respected in the government marketplace and understands that in spite of the 1,600 plus pages of Federal Acquisition Regulations it's about RELATIONSHIPS!!! Mark tells you in plain English how to go about the process of business development. Except for NASA, this is not rocket science, . . . it's about following the proven path successful entrepreneurs have used to create market share."

—Scott Denniston, Former Director; Office of Small Business and
Center for Veterans Enterprise, Dept. of Veterans Affairs,
and Founder/President of the Scott Group of Virginia

"When I was presented with the opportunity of reading an advance copy of Mark Amtower's latest book, *Selling to the Government*, I was both honored and, of course, intensely interested. . . . [T]his is a topic of considerable relevance and even controversy in the realms of public sector procurement.

Mark did not disappoint, as his text displayed a rare balance between meaningful experience and practical expertise, delivering much needed insight into an area in which a clear line of both vision and understanding is—more often than not—obfuscated by contradictory policies and competing interests. Explained using informative as well as entertaining anecdotal references, this is a cover-to-cover read . . . probably in one sitting.

My advice . . . buy the book and enjoy, then prosper!"

—Jon Hansen, Author and the Host of the PI Window on Business Show

"I've witnessed Mark Amtower in action on his home turf in Washington, DC—he's a certified genius about marketing and selling to the government. In this book, he shares his secrets. Mark shows you that making money (lots of it) selling to the government doesn't need to be mysterious and you'll learn exactly what you need to do to succeed."

—David Meerman Scott, Best-Selling Author of *The New Rules of Marketing* and Coauthor of *Marketing Lessons from the Grateful Dead*

"Mark Amtower has been the go-to guy for marketing to the federal government for more years than I can remember. *Selling to the Government* distills his decades of experience in marketing to the government into a book you can buy for a few bucks. It's the bargain of the century!"

—Bob Bly, Copywriter

"I have been observing Mark Amtower and his successful clients for over twenty years, and there is no one—and I mean no one—who knows more about successfully selling to the government than Mark. He is the 'Dean of Government Marketing.'"

—Don Libey, CEO, Libey LLC, and Veteran Direct Marketing Advisor

"This book is a must for anyone selling to the government. Amtower gives you the answers you need to questions you don't know you have. He will help you put the puzzle together—in a way that works for your specific situation—in this engaging guide to selling to the world's largest customer.

—David Powell, COO, Federal Business Council, Inc.

"Don't be seduced by the big numbers of the government market. As Amtower and his cast of B2G experts explain, success takes time, persistence and understanding, the basic workings of this unique market. The public sector landscape is littered with companies who thought they had the right product or service, only to fail because they didn't understand how the market worked. Amtower's premise is one that everyone from the C-suite to the new recruit should heed—never forget the blocking and tackling of the government market."

—Nick Wakeman, Editor-in-Chief, *Washington Technology*

"Mark Amtower's *Selling to the Government* volume is a useful guide for getting started and succeeding in the government marketplace. There are plenty of tips and comprehensive information in the report that businesses large and small can use to tap the world's largest market for goods and services. Chapter 11 on Web 2.0 tools shows that Mark has his eye on the future of government contracting. Executives eager to get their share of government contracts should have Mark's volume on their bookshelves."

—Michael Keating, Senior Editor, *Government Product News*

"Mark Amtower is known as the guy who knows everybody and has devoted a lifetime to earning the bold title 'Government Market Master.' However, one of the things that impresses me most about Mark is not the encyclopedic knowledge you'll find in this book, but his humility to keep on learning and growing. An expert at traditional networking and research, Mark is also well known in the Gov 2.0 community for his voracious appetite for new media, his critical eye on social networking and Internet fads, and his willingness to embrace change. This book represents not only Mark's three-decade history in learning the government markets, but also his best lessons of today and his contagious attitude for staying at the top of the game."

—Adriel Hampton, Producer and Cofounder, Gov 2.0 Radio

"What Zig Ziglar is to selling, Mark Amtower is to government marketing. He is a master of his domain and can break it down and teach it like no other. Don't waste time and money trying to enter the government market blind. Let Mark Amtower's book *Selling to the Government* be the guide as you traverse this unmapped, but lucrative territory."

—Steve Ressler, Founder and President, GovLoop.com

"So many businesses think they can't benefit from selling to the government. The executives of those businesses apparently never met Mark Amtower. Helping organizations sell profitably to the federal government isn't simply Mark's area of considerable expertise; it's also his passion. As an editor for several trade publications dedicated to marketing, I've long relied on Mark for the skinny on reaching this massive, complex audience, and he's never failed to come through with up-to-date, actionable, and easy-to-understand (and often entertaining!) advice. The bottom line: If you're considering selling your goods or services to the federal government, Mark's your go-to source."

—Sherry Chiger, Editor-at-Large, Chief Marketer, Director, Multichannel Merchant

"This is the perfect book to understand how to do business with the government. Mark makes what seems so obvious to federal employees understandable to those who want and need to do business in the federal market space. I would recommend that those already doing business with the federal government should read this book as well. Mark provides tremendous insight into the federal market."

—Karen Evans, Partner, National Director for the U.S. Cyber Challenge, and former Administrator, E-Government, and Information Technology, Executive Office of the President, Office of Management and Budget

"If you are selling to government (or hope to), you need to read this book! Actually, don't just read it. Do as Mark suggests: Highlight it, mark it up, and keep it for reference. It's a keeper."

—Ann Handley, Chief Content Officer, MarketingProfs and coauthor of *Content Rules*

"It's rare that a guy who makes his living as a consultant will give away his experience in a book. Here, you're getting Mark's 30 years of wisdom in how to sell to government buyers. Grab it now!"

—Ruth P. Stevens, president, eMarketing Strategy, and Adjunct Professor, Columbia Business School

"Mark Amtower is an object lesson in B2G marketing. He lives his words. Because he practices the basics, he defies the odds and continues to make a successful career in a difficult space. His longevity in the federal market proves his value; he's been there, he's seen it, he has the knowledge to draw the detailed map of the calm but deep waters of selling to the federal government."

—Lisa Wolfe, Program Director, Federal News Radio 1500 AM, Washington, DC

"The federal government really is Fortune 1 and can be a great source of revenue for most companies for decades. However, it's a market that requires understanding, patience, and most of all, commitment. Amtower's new book answers many questions for companies considering entering the market and solid tips for companies that are already entrenched around the Beltway."

—Fred Diamond, DIAMOND Marketing

"Once again, Mark provides a veritable treasure trove of relevant, actionable information useful to novices and veterans of B2G alike! Unless you are winning every possible piece of business in your segment of the government marketplace, take the time to read this book. Your competition will."

—Guy Timberlake, Chief Visionary Officer, The American Small Business Coalition

"If you want expert advice about selling to the government, Mark is your guy, and this is the book. Whether you're a newcomer seeking to enter the government market or a veteran looking for a refresher, Mark's book covers the basics, debunks the myths and shares his best tips to help you find the right path to success in the government market."

—Brian Halligan, CEO of HubSpot and Best-Selling Author of *Inbound Marketing* and Coauthor of *Marketing Lessons from the Grateful Dead*

"*Selling to the Government* provides a clear understanding to the process of selling to the government. Mark provides readers with a strong foundation to successfully sell to the government. I read Warren Buffett to learn about investing and Mark Amtower to learn how to sell to the government. Both Warren and Mark understand the benefit of simplifying the truly complex."

—Andrew Meringoff, Founder, Government Connections

"If you are serious about being successful in the business of doing business with the government sector, Mark is a must-read author. Once again Mark gives us an easy to understand, direct, incredibly practical, and useful guide to doing business with the government. Mark has probably forgotten more about doing business in this sector than most of us can remember at any point in time. He has made it his business to get it right and help others succeed in a very complicated, yet simple market. Whether you are looking to get into the government market or hoping to be more successful in it, Mark's advice will make a huge difference—if you follow it. Corporate leaders and stakeholders in other businesses should be as fortunate as we are in the government contracting business to have an advisor as wise and as practical as Mark Amtower to help them succeed."

—Cal Hackeman, National Managing Partner, Technology Industry Practice, Grant Thornton LLP

"The insider knowledge and shortcuts described in this book will save those new to the government contracting industry precious bid and proposal time and dollars."

—Brenda Crist, President, Association of Proposal Management Professionals, National Capital Chapter

"Amtower's *Selling to the Government* is infused with his expertise, wit, and practical know-how. This informative and entertaining book should be required reading for anyone selling to government. Mark truly understands that to achieve success, a company must be fully committed to the public market sector, take all of the right steps to comprehend and respond to the needs and requirements of its customers, and ultimately deliver the right internal structures, contracts, relationships, and people to get the job done. Even the most seasoned government sellers will benefit from reading this book as ongoing education, constant fine-tuning, and refinement of technique are key to long term success."

—Christina V. Rother, President, CDW Government LLC

"The federal government market is the largest single market in our country. Mark Amtower's book opens the door for readers on how to approach this maze of complex rules and procedures, including its opportunities and pitfalls. It is a "must read" for any company or individual doing business with the federal government."

—Dr Andrew Uscher, Director of Corporate Relations, Senior Executives Association

"Mark Amtower's book provides readers with valuable information about the federal marketplace. His insights about federal contacting are based on his long experience in this field and are especially useful to anyone who wants to approach the complex federal market."

—Carol Bonosaro, President, Senior Executive Association

SELLING
TO THE
GOVERNMENT

What It Takes to Compete and Win
in the World's Largest Market

MARK AMTOWER

WILEY

John Wiley & Sons, Inc.

Published by John Wiley & Sons, Inc., Hoboken, New Jersey.
Published simultaneously in Canada.

For general information on our other products and services or for technical support, please
contact our Customer Care Department within the United States at (800) 762-2974,
outside the United States at (317) 572-3993 or fax (317) 572-4002.

Wiley also publishes its books in a variety of electronic formats. Some content that appears
in print may not be available in electronic books. For more information about Wiley
products, visit our web site at www.wiley.com.

ISBN 978-0-470-88133-0 (cloth)
ISBN 978-0-470-93382-4 (ebk)
ISBN 978-0-470-93384-8 (ebk)
ISBN 978-0-470-93386-2 (ebk)

Printed in the United States of America

10 9 8 7 6 5 4 3 2 1

To my wife, Mary Ellen, who is a constant inspiration and a great partner in every respect; and to my children, Elora and Travis, who tolerate my strange work habits and love me anyway.

CONTENTS

FOREWORD

As those of us in and around the Beltway know, government contracting can be a very good place to be. In this book, *Selling to the Government*, Mark Amtower shows what it really takes to break into the government market.

There are many things one must know, much infrastructure to get into place, and lots of buyoff required from senior management in order for the real commitment necessary to break through the red tape, the market intricacies, and the overall "bigness" of this market. There are many relationships that must be established, regardless of where your company is located, if you want to do business with the government.

Many of TechAmerica's 1,200 member companies are ensconced in the government market, and as the largest and strongest voice and resource for technology in the country, we help our companies navigate this vast government market, federal civilian and Department of Defense, as well as state and local government. To do this, we have a seasoned, well-connected staff; the importance of this is something Mark Amtower reminds us of constantly: *relationships*.

The learning curve for those entering the government market is long and slow, and there are few legitimate shortcuts.

There are books on getting a General Services Administration Schedule and on winning contracts, and there is even Mark's first book on marketing to the government, *Government*

Marketing Best Practices (2005). What has been lacking is the "big picture" book: one that outlines the corporate commitment necessary to enter the market intelligently, the infrastructure required once in, the staffing requirements to pursue bids, and much more.

With this new book, *Selling to the Government: What It Takes to Compete and Win in the World's Largest Market*, Mark Amtower fills in this missing link. It is the first book to address what it takes from a corporate point of view to enter the market slowly and intelligently and to build an organization capable of playing in the big leagues.

In his trademark, straightforward style, Amtower lays out the requirements and warns readers up front that although anyone can play, most will end up walking away. Long known for his candor, he clearly lays the process out for anyone willing to pay the entry fee: working long hours, doing months of groundwork, staffing, managing infrastructural issues involving accounting and legal concerns, handling the glacial nature of the government market, learning to market and sell to the government, and so much more.

Our executive vice president for the public sector, Olga Grkavac, commented on the cover of Mark's first book: "Mark Amtower is a true original." Some things don't change.

—Phil Bond, Chief Executive Officer,
TechAmerica

PREFACE

Korean Tae Kwan Do master Jhoon Rhee once said there are only seven basic moves to Tae Kwan Do, and everything else is a combination of those seven moves. He taught his students to practice the basics daily, even those who had attained various degrees of black belt. His point: It is always about the basics.

My mentor in the government market, Lynn Bateman, taught me the basics in government contracting, and she told me to stay current on those basics. She taught me where I could get the best information and instructed me to monitor those sources for the nuanced (read: slow) changes that would occur. She taught all her students, even those winning and managing major contracts, to stay current on the basics.

We all need to know and practice the basics.

Let's start with a simple premise—my variation of the Pareto principle. Ninety-five percent of businesspeople out there are happy with where they are, who they are, and what they currently know. They assume that by some form of osmosis, by going to work, or some other proximity to thought and intelligent action, they will get smarter. Possible, but not practical.

Four percent of people out there take some type of action on a semiregular basis to get better at whatever they do. They read the trade publications, attend meetings, and network regularly. Practical and good.

One percent of the people out there wish to excel at what they do and read professional books, journals, and trade publications; join pertinent groups; attend seminars and webinars; and find multiple ways to share and grow. Difficult, doable, and a major differentiator.

Welcome to the top 5 percent bracket. You opened this book.

On what do I base this premise? In my 28 years of studying the business-to-government (B2G) market, I have observed that about 90 percent or more of the companies that try to enter the government market fail. They fail not from lack of skill at what they do; they fail from lack of understanding the nuances of a new market—a different market—with rules arcane enough to cover literally tens of thousands of pages of "government-speak." They do not adapt. Our extensive glossary in Appendix 1 will help you with "gov-speak."

Appendix 2 will give you some great leads for publications and associations that serve the market. Updated information for the book will be available at www.GovernmentMarketMaster .com; just click on the book cover.

I am a student of the government market and have been for nearly 30 years. I am also a legitimate Government Market Master. I am a master of *one aspect* of the market—marketing—but that is not the only thing that makes me a Government Market Master. The other facet of being a Government Market Master is knowing who *the masters of the other facets* of the market are and having strong relationships with them. There are many pieces to the puzzle, and without all the pieces, the picture is never complete. So, I keep studying, and I keep finding people who are really good at the other parts of the puzzle.

The first sentence of my first book, *Government Marketing Best Practices*, is, "This market—any market—is about relationships."

Throughout the course of this book, you will meet many of those I consider to be masters of their pieces of this puzzle; the people who comprise my inner circle; and professionals who understand their respective niches like few others in this market. Together, we will share with you tips, tricks, ideas, resources, and more that will help you along your path to becoming a master of your piece of this market. These are the people I rely on to fill in the blanks in my skill sets. You need to find similar people to rely on to help you succeed in this vast and potentially confusing market. The quality of those advising you will be reflected in your outcome. You will also find advice from some of my advisors in Appendix 3.

But don't look for shortcuts. There are none, and those who tell you there are shortcuts are selling you pipe dreams. There are charlatans in every market, but you will find none in this book. The only real "shortcut" is market knowledge applied to your daily actions.

So, for you business owners, presidents, chief-level executives (C-levels), and board members reading this, do not take this lightly. Heed the advice from me and my inner circle of Government Market Masters and you have a real chance for success here in Global One—the U.S. government market.

Finally, this book is not a panacea for all aspects of selling to the government. This book is the *beginning of your journey* and is designed to direct you to other valuable resources and alert you to the many things you will encounter along the way: the good, the bad, and the ugly.

There are many ways to succeed in the government market, and each path is different. This book can help you determine the best path for your ultimate success. I have been studying and working in this market a long time, picking some of the brightest brains in this business, and the results are here, waiting for *you*.

So, sit back with a highlighter, notepad, and pencil, and let's see how we can take you from B2G novice to B2G black belt—a true Government Market Master!

And a final quote from my first book: "The government market is only sexy if you like money."

HOW TO READ THIS BOOK

Every book is different in its design and intentions. This book is designed to be a guide for the novice and a refresher for the professional. For the novice, it is sequential, and for those more experienced, each chapter may be a refresher or may provide new insights on a specific topic. Chapter 11, "The Missing Link: Web 2.0 Tools," deals with social networking and Web 2.0 tools and will be good for both the experienced market professional and the novice. This book is meant to be used as a reference, so I hope you come back to it again and again. Keep in mind that updated information will always be available on the Web site, www.GovernmentMarketMaster.com.

I suggest you read this book with a highlighter, Post-it flags, and a small notebook at hand. Highlighting key passages in a book is a great way to reinforce an idea you find useful.

I use Post-it flags to mark the most memorable and useful passages in the books I read. For those same books, the ones rife with useful ideas, I keep a notebook handy so that I can make a to-do list of all the actions I need to take as a result of reading.

All Web references, recommended companies, contact information for those quoted, and updates or changes will be available at www.GovernmentMarketMaster.com; just click on the book cover on the home page.

DISCLAIMER

The government market is different in many respects, and it is highly nuanced.

Please keep in mind that the government market changes—generally slowly, but it does change. The information in this book is somewhat granular, but it needs to be verified with the resources we reference throughout the book. The government Web sites change, but we will keep them current at www.GovernmentMarketMaster.com.

You need advice from experienced professionals (legal, accounting, contracting) on all aspects of doing business with the government in order to be successful in this B2G market, and you need it early in the process. Do not rely on your business-to-business (B2B) attorney or accountant when dealing with matters concerning doing business with the government. Some of those I recommend will be linked at the Web site as well.

Further, if you have a B2B advertising agency or public relations firm, they, too, will indicate that they can perform the B2G marketing and public relations. This is not accurate. Our list of recommended marketing firms and consultants will be available at the Web site, www.GovernmentMarket Master.com.

Finally, my contact information will be there as well. Feel free to drop me a line.

ACKNOWLEDGMENTS

There are too many people to whom I owe a debt of gratitude to enumerate here, so a short list will have to suffice. No one makes it without help in this market.

To my mentor, Lynn Bateman, who taught a generation (or two) how to navigate the rules, regulations, and red tape so that we can make a living in this arcane market, and to my friend Tom Hewitt, who remains the most connected person I know in this market.

To my friends, advisors, business associates, and all those whose help I rely on: David Powell of the Federal Business Council; Richard Mackey of CapitalReps; Michael Balsam of Onvia; Peter Long of MCH; Michael Keating of Penton Media; Lisa Wolfe and all the show hosts and staff at Federal News Radio; Ralph Drybrough and Rob Sanchez of MeritDirect; Courtney Fairchild of Global Services; Jim Garlow, Lisa DeLuca, and Ann-Marie Clark of CDW; Mark Meudt and Ludmilla Parnell of GDIT; Guy Timberlake of the American Small Business Coalition; Phil Bond and Olga Grkavac of TechAmerica; Ken Allen of ACT/IAC; Alan Balutis of Cisco; Dendy Young of McLean Capitol; Bob Davis of MilVets; Jae Collins of Prime Solutions; Anne Armstrong and Nick Wakeman of 1105; Judy Bradt of Summit Insight; Tom Carroll and the crew at Carroll Publications; Jim Shanahan and Lee Kramer of FTS; Larry Allen of the Coalition for

Government Procurement; Joan Daly of Daly Associates; Hope Lane and the team at Aronson & Company; Ardell Fleeson of CBRE and the doyen of D.C. networking; Eva Neumann and the crew at ENC; Evan Weisel of Welz & Weisel; Lisa Dezzutti of Market Connections; Fred Diamond of Diamond Marketing; and my buddy, Suzanne Kubota of WFED.

Finally, to my friends at John Wiley & Sons, Inc.— Shannon Vargo, Elana Schulman, and Lauren Freestone—who made my work look good, and to David Meerman Scott for introducing me to Shannon and Wiley.

Omissions are unintentional, and there will be another book. . . .

CHAPTER I

What It Takes to Play

Tips and Caveats for Chief Executive Officers, Boards, and Others Looking for Shortcuts

A TALE OF TWO COMPANIES

By all appearances, it was the best of times. The late 1990s was a time of loose money, grandiose business plans, and the fervent belief that things were only going to get better—forever. Start-ups were being funded on what seemed to be whims. In the words of Alan Greenspan, it was a time of "irrational exuberance." Nowhere did this seem more apparent than in the staid business-to-government (B2G) arena.

Out of the literally hundreds of B2G start-ups from that time, two stand out in my mind: eFederal and PlanetGov.

PlanetGov had a business plan that apparently ran on for hundreds of pages, but the gist was to be all things possible to the feds, including a one-stop shop for all products and services. They wanted to provide information for federal employees on retirement, promotions, investments (the government 401(k) program), and other jobs, and oh, by the way, products and services, too—absolutely everything under one roof; no need to look elsewhere. They even hired top government reporter Mike Causey from the *Washington Post*, hired editors and reporters from trade journals, and set out to build the biggest Web site with the most bells and whistles imaginable.

Ambitious, to say the least.

On the other hand, eFederal wanted to be the first completely virtual store for the federal market, initially targeting the SmartPay (the federal credit card) market for micro-purchases (at that time, anything under $2,500), then migrating up to higher-end products.

Then came the dot-bomb crash, and eFederal was among the early casualties. They and their venture capital (VC) backers assumed the feds would line up for the convenience of an online shopping experience. However, the government is not known as an early adopter, and the reticence of government credit card holders to buy off Web sites (at that time) was still high.

The assumption of eFederal was a fatal flaw in their business plan. Shopping online with a government credit card was not a given, and there were many valid restrictions in place, among them the security of the shopping experience. Fads, even trends, outside the government market should not be used as building blocks for penetrating the government market. Even if they are adopted, it will be on "government time": glacial.

PlanetGov represents a different outcome. The core plan was to pursue government business in the traditional way, bidding on contracts that fit the skills of the company. The bells and whistles were jettisoned, the company had some significant layoffs (18 of the 20 reporters and editors were let go in December 2000), and PlanetGov regrouped and focused on the real business of government.

PlanetGov's core business allowed it to emerge as a significant player in the government market, rapidly becoming a top-50 contractor according to *Washington Technology*. In July 2004, PlanetGov changed its name to Apptis, adopted from the company's slogan, "Applying Technologies, Inspiring Solutions." For the 2010 fiscal year (FY), Apptis was ranked number 35 among *Washington Technology*'s top 100 contractors.

PlanetGov/Apptis jettisoned the dot-com−era flash and got down to the core business, pursuing government contracts and building deep relationships with key customers and partners.

In good times or bad, one must grasp how the government operates before making a play to enter the market. If you predicate your growth on unrealistic assumptions, things that have occurred elsewhere, or things that are predicted to occur, you are doomed from the outset.

BASICS

This book is a "basics" book—the things you need to know if you are new to the market or to be reminded of occasionally, even if you are a veteran. I wrote this book for companies entering the government market, but government market veterans can and will relearn from it as well. This is an introduction for chief-level (C-level) executives in companies of any size, from home-based mom-and-pop operations to multibillion-dollar-plus enterprises. It is designed to deliver much of the pertinent information you need to understand how to successfully enter the government marketplace. I would like to say it delivers all of the information you need, but that is a claim beyond my capabilities. However, I draw upon the expertise of many of my advisors and colleagues throughout this book, people who are masters of many of the knowledge niches we'll discuss.

For over 12 years, I have offered a research program on successfully entering the federal market that is designed to help companies make the go-no-go decision and lay out their initial market penetration plan. It is a multistep process, where

I provide research on the market potential for your product or service, including the following:

- The General Services Administration (GSA) spending for the specific product or service for the last three years. I use the GSA Schedule as a market barometer.

- A list of your top competitors and what they make. This provides a "food chain" view of the market.

- The visibility your company has in the government market, as measured by the Google government search tool (which searches only government Web sites) and by searching other pertinent Web sites or industry publications. Being known in your niche is important, and occasionally measuring your visibility is a good thing to benchmark.

- An analysis of the "government friendliness" of your Web site, making certain your Web site, a primary information portal, is designed to attract government visitors.

- A glossary of the right "gov-speak" phrases to attract government buyers. The government uses its own language, which you will see as we proceed. If you don't speak it, you will have a much harder time entering the market.

- Who the buyers are for your products and services. Once I see what you sell, I can make a determination—an educated guess—on who the audience is for those products or services. This allows you to target your message to a much tighter community.

- Recommendations on how to sell, which contracts would work best for you, and why.

- The type of personnel required to pursue government business. Your current staff may be excellent for the markets you pursue but may not be a great fit for the government market.

- A realistic assessment of your chances of growing a successful government business if you dedicate the right resources.

This book will show you how I do this research and more. I will be more than happy to accept payment from you to perform this research on your behalf, but I'd be happier to have you call me in 6, 12, or 18 months and say, "Hey, Mark, I used that book and we have some great new government customers."

However, do not expect immediate results from the government market. You have to give yourself a window of 12 to 24 months in order to gain any traction here. That is your first big lesson.

The scope of what you need to know varies somewhat from niche to niche and can depend on the size and ownership of your company. But the B2G market entry *knowledge base* required is basically the same, regardless of your product or niche. There are many things you must *understand and accept* before attempting to enter this market, and these will be outlined in some detail here.

The U.S. government market represents the largest single market in the world. It is truly Global One. Government contract tracking firm Onvia estimates that government business—federal, state, local, and education—represents over 45 percent of the gross domestic product (GDP). Read that last part again: over 45 percent of the GDP. If you exchanged "revenue" for "sales," many states, counties, and municipalities would replace more than half of the *Fortune* 1,000 list. Federal agencies would dominate the top 25.

The government market is a *huge* market, and anyone can play in it. But not everyone will, and of those who do, most will not succeed.

Why?

Most companies come in with unrealistic expectations predicated on second- and thirdhand knowledge, bad advice, and little or no adult supervision. They fail quickly and blame it on anything but their own ignorance.

It is not that you have to know *all* this stuff, but you need the right resources available to tell you which parts are germane to *your* success. And you have to be able to adapt your organization to the way business is done in the B2G arena. It will not adapt to you.

The importance of being adaptable for a manufacturer entering the government market is the focus of our first vignette from a market veteran, shared by Dendy Young, former chief executive officer (CEO) of GTSI. Dendy is a long-time friend, former CEO of two government resellers, market veteran and expert, and the first CEO to meet with me, going back to 1991.

DOING BUSINESS WITH THE GOVERNMENT REQUIRES A LOT OF LISTENING

When Panasonic Corporation wanted to enter the personal computer (PC) marketplace in the early 1990s, they knew they could not just walk in and compete with Dell, HP, Compaq, IBM, and the rest.

So, they differentiated: They created a PC laptop that was more rugged and reliable than anything else out there. They called it the CF-22, and they gave it a rugged magnesium case.

I was at GTSI Corp at the time when they asked us to carry the product. They realized that we had the contracts and the customer relationships and the sales force and that we needed something to sell. They had the CF-22, a product that should be well suited to military use.

So, we worked with them to market and promote the product. We wanted them to brand their product: To give it a catchy name and spend time and money on promoting it. They came up with the name "ToughBook," which seemed like a good fit. We added it to all our contracts, we invested heavily by training our sales force and our support organization, and we demonstrated it directly to customers and at every tabletop show and symposium.

We were constantly asking Panasonic for changes: Some of our customers wanted the product to be more rugged; some wanted it to be more elegant, but still rugged. Others wanted it to be smaller, and some wanted it to be lighter or less expensive. Panasonic was very attentive to our requests: They would bring engineers to Washington to listen for themselves, and they would let us show our customers prototypes to get feedback. Slowly, in time, they added new models that responded to our customers' requests until, within seven or eight years, they had a broad and very responsive product line.

In time, as the revenues grew, Panasonic expanded their own support organization to include more channel support and business development. However, they never lost their commitment to the channel. Their revenues grew into the hundreds of millions of dollars in the government sector.

In all, it was a very successful partnership for both Panasonic and GTSI.

WE'RE TALKING COMPETITIVE

As of March 23, 2010, there were 591,988 active registrants in the central contractor registration program, available at www .ccr.gov, the official Web site where companies register to do business with the federal government. In good or bad economic times, hundreds of companies look to enter the government market every week. In bad times, this activity picks up, as the government market seems to represent a safe haven—the only recession-proof market segment.

Let's simply start with the scope of the market we are addressing, the U.S. government market: federal, state, local, and education, or for those semiconversant in gov-speak, Fed and SLED.

Go to www.ccr.gov for the latest number of active registrants.

MARKET STATS AND FACTS

According to the government contract tracking firm Onvia, the U.S. government market represents nearly 50 percent of the GDP and is comprised of nearly 90,000 separate governmental entities:

- 3,034 counties
- 19,429 municipalities
- 16,504 townships
- 35,052 special district governments
- 13,506 school districts
- 512 Native American nations
- 50 states
- 1 District of Columbia
- 6 U.S. territories
- 1 U.S. federal government

Total: 88,095

Many of these governmental units would qualify for the *Fortune* 100 list. There are states, cities, and counties that spend more than some major corporations.

Buildings and facilities: On the federal side alone, there are over 37,000 occupied office sites (buildings and individual offices) in the continental United States (CONUS in gov-speak). This does not include any military or U.S. postal facilities.

Doing research on a presentation for the Modular Building Institute in 2008, I discovered the building activity at federal, state, and local levels is virtually nonstop. With the military Base Realignment and Closure (BRAC) program in full swing, the activity in and around the bases being eliminated and the bases gaining activity will be with us for several years to come.

Fleet: Government fleet activity is huge. Don't think simply ships for "fleet," which includes any vehicle that runs on land, air, or sea. When I spoke to the National Truck Equipment Association in 2008, my federal research found the following:

- Trucks/truck tractors: 380,765
- Trailers and semitrailers: 4,792
- Buses: 5,499
- Automobiles: 110,339

For the same presentation, the research for state and local government found the following:

- Trucks: 1,822,210
- Trailers and semitrailers: 252,953
- Buses: 470,055
- Automobiles: 1,265,456

This research was largely based on Michael Keating's annual *Keating Report on Government Spending*. Michael is senior editor and top researcher for Penton Media's GovPro Group (www.govpro.com), which publishes *Government Product News* among other magazines for the public sector. I also utilize Onvia (www.onvia.com) statistics supplied by Michael Balsam, the chief knowledge officer at Onvia. Both Penton and Onvia provide great research and actionable data. I use both every time I am conducting research for an article, book, or presentation.

Employment: According to a 2007 report from the U.S. Census Bureau, one in eight adults employed on a full-time basis is employed by some level of government, and almost 20 million full-time employees (FTEs in gov-speak) work at some level of government. These people represent every discipline you can think of, from research scientists to welders, white collar and blue collar, janitorial services to executives, and everything in between.

Products and services spending: The U.S. government market buys every legitimate business product and service imaginable— and many consumer products as well. The federal market alone spends more than $600 billion annually for these products and services. When you add in the state, local, and education markets, we are approaching *$2 trillion*.

SmartPay credit card spending: In FY 2009, the federal government used the SmartPay card for nearly $30 billion of purchases. The categories for the purchases are fleet (all things vehicle related), travel expenses (the first government credit card was the Diners Club card, which was exclusively for travel), and small purchases. Of these, the small purchases accounted for nearly $20 billion, with fleet accounting for over $6 billion and travel over $3 billion. Some cards are used for more than one category of purchase.

The *GSA Schedules* (discussed in more depth in Chapter 2) provide an overview of the breadth and depth of products purchased by the federal government. If you sell a business product or service—and even many consumer products—you probably have an audience here.

Any way you slice it, it's a big market. And when you are on the outside looking in, the U.S. government market is perhaps the most intimidating market anywhere.

So, why aren't you doing business with the government right now? If you are not doing business with the government, it is usually because of one of two reasons: either you've never tried because of what you've heard or you tried it once and got burned—maybe badly. In either case, your market approach, or market avoidance, was probably caused by market myths.

GOVERNMENT MARKET MYTHS

Most markets have myths, rumors, and other semiplausible informational tidbits surrounding them. There are myths that keep companies out of the market and myths that bring them in. Each can be equally harmful. Myths that keep you out are simply making you leery for the wrong reasons; myths that bring you in are usually those that scream easy money.

Regardless, the myths abound for every market, and the government market is no different. There have always been myths and semitruths floating around about doing business with the government, so let's dispense with a few of them right now. Throughout the book, we will find other myths and dispense with them as well.

On the side of never having tried government, these are the most recurrent myths:

Myth 1: *The government market is too big, and we can't do it.* The government market is big, but it is not a single, homogeneous market. Rather, it is a quagmire of niches: information technology, office supplies, hospital equipment, fleet (land, sea, and air), finance, facilities, agriculture, environmental—you name it, it is probably in here. If you ferret out your niche, you will start to find your comfort zone—people who speak your language (well, sort of) and share your background. Niche it down and you'll find your sweet spot.

Myth 2: *Government contracts are wired. If you don't use the right people, you'll never get the work.* Wired bids are a thing of the past. There is a transparency in the U.S. government market that does not exist elsewhere, and wired bids are largely out. That does not mean that congressional earmarks are a thing of the past, but these are different than contracts. As for knowing the right people, this part is true in every market. Knowing the right people in any market can give you leverage, and this market is no different. However, there is nothing stopping *you* from meeting the right people as you grow your knowledge base.

Myth 3: *The government demands the lowest price, and we can't afford that.* The government strives to save the taxpayers money on most contracts, but it does not always work out that way. If you enter the market without sufficient guidance, you may end up offering products and services at prices so low, you will never make a profit. If there is a service component to your offering, there is always room for profit. With the proper help, you will find that a good living can be made in this market. Otherwise, there would not be so many companies here.

On the side of "I've tried it and failed," we have these myths:

Myth 4: *We have a great product; resellers will line up to sell our stuff.* I have never been approached by a company that stated, "I have a crappy product . . ." Everyone, it seems, has a unique product, the best, the cutting edge, or has a brand name behind it that is bound to drive hordes of feds into a buying frenzy. This is wrong in all instances. The government buys products that are commercially viable—proven elsewhere. Name brands do not matter in the government market, and the smart resellers line up for products with a track record and companies behind the products that can and will help drive sales. When a name brand sells here, they have earned the right to do so.

Myth 5: *A GSA Schedule ("number") makes the cash register ring.* There are many misconceptions about what a GSA Schedule is and what it does for you. This is among my favorites, and this myth survives in spite of vast evidence to the contrary. Of the 12,000-plus companies on the GSA, at least 2,000 make zero dollars. While the GSA Schedule can be a part of your go-to-market plan, it requires salespeople skilled in selling from a Schedule to leverage it properly.

Myth 6: *The government has set-asides for small businesses, so we're bound to find easy work.* Many companies assume their small business status (small, disadvantaged, minority owned, veteran owned, woman owned, etc.) will guarantee them a contract; all you have to do is show your credentials at the small business office and the work is yours. Nothing could be further from the truth, and few things irritate small business officers in the government as much as companies making this assumption. First, you have to have something to sell that the government wants. Your business status comes later.

There are other myths, but these seem to be among the most recurrent.

MARKET GUARANTEES

Then, there are those seeking guarantees. Over the years, I have had numerous calls, especially from small business owners, asking for proposals. After they review the proposal, I will get a call from some staff person. This staffer has been tasked with asking me what guarantees I can provide that my advice will lead to winning contracts from our favorite uncle.

As you have probably guessed by now, there are no guarantees here any more than there are anywhere else, so that is what I tell them. What I really want to say is that if they find someone who does guarantee them business (and there are several of those out there), they will end up as another chalk outline on the sidewalk of the government market.

What I can guarantee is that for those of you who read this book, take some notes, figure out where you fit in this market, and follow the advice that applies to you, your chances of success are a hundredfold higher. Period.

Bob Davis, a business development professional in the government market and long-time Amtower advisor, made one of the most telling statements when I interviewed him for a CD set we recorded in 2007: *Market share is rented, never owned.*

The ultimate guarantee is that there isn't one.

So, Mr. or Ms. CEO, what's first for you?

MARKET RESEARCH

Some basic market research is always best, and some of this you can, and should, do yourself. Basic research for me starts with, "Is there a way for me to make money in this market?" I want to see if traction is going to occur or if I will simply be spinning my wheels. Simple enough, right? You need to familiarize yourself with the market and start the educational process.

I think it is important for executives to know how to do some basic research on their own for several reasons, not the least of which is to verify what you may hear from outside or internal sources that may not have it right. Many people providing data on the B2G market are using older, oft-repeated information, and a few just make it up as they go along, assuming no one will check the facts.

There are several excellent sources for research in the B2G market—many paid; others free. There is good free research that you can do on your own. Doing it yourself will pay both near-term and long-term dividends. In fact, there is useful information available on most U.S. government Web sites that can help you when you are planning to enter the government market. There has always been a fair amount of publicly available information if you know *how and where* to look.

Among these are the trade publications for the government market, the few books published on doing business with the government, trade associations, meetings with government personnel (executives and managers, contracting and procurement officers, small business officers), many research firms willing and able to provide custom research (some better than others), and government Web sites (a good list of the useful government Web sites can be found at www.GovernmentExpress.com on the "Resources" page).

Among the trade publications on my regular reading list are *Washington Technology, Federal Computer Week, Government Executive, Government Computer News, Public Manager, Governing, Government Product News, Government Procurement, American City and County, Government Security, Government Fleet*, and a few others. Often, I will scan these at their respective Web sites. Select those that fit your niche, and find the other publications that do as well. Share the most germane articles with key staffers. This does two things: It informs the staff of good information, and it tells them you are on top of the game.

There are many associations that are directly or indirectly involved with government business, and I try to mention several in the associated appendix, but here are a few to give you an idea: the Armed Forces Communications and Electronics Association (AFCEA), the American Council for Technology and its Industry Advisory Council (ACT/IAC), TechAmerica, the Professional Services Council, the American Small Business Coalition (ASBC), the International Facilities Management Association, Women in Technology, and many more. Each of these is worthwhile in its own right, and when you find the association or special interest group that works for you, then join it. Join with the idea of participating. I will address this in more detail later.

There are also hundreds of Web sites with solid information—too many to list here. We will list some of the best in the related appendix.

The best known way to sell to the federal government is through the GSA Schedules (Myth 5, right?). The GSA Schedules will be discussed in length in Chapter 3, but basically, they are a set of government contracts (41 in all) that segments what the government buys into categories. Companies apply for and negotiate a GSA Schedule contract so that they have a contractual vehicle through which to sell.

In all, there are over 20,000 GSA Schedule contracts (many companies have multiple GSA Schedules)—hundreds, if not thousands, for each of the 41 categories. Before you enter the market, you need to be able to see what kind of money happens in your category through this popular contract. This will be a barometer for you to measure your potential in the market, and later, to measure your growth.

To find out who is making what on the GSA, I use the GSA Schedule Sales Query (SSQ) tool, available at http://ssq .gsa.gov.

Here's how you use it. When you go to this page, simply click on "Create Report" from the menu on the left-hand side. This will take you to a form that asks for your name, company name, and so forth. Don't fill this out; just click on "Proceed." This will take you to a page with 11 report options. I normally focus on number 10—"Total by Contractor for a Specific Schedule and Fiscal Year." So, I select that and click on "Generate Report."

You need to know the Schedule you are searching for, because the screen will then ask you to select which Schedule you want a report for. Go to Chapter 3 to see which Schedule you fit in.

Now, you need to select the FY and the report format, for which there are three options: "Text File for Importing," "Text File for Printing," or "Excel Spreadsheet." I always choose "Excel Spreadsheet." Then, I click "Create Report." On the next screen, you are asked to read the disclaimer and approve. Do so. If you don't accept, you don't get the report.

Depending on the report size (some are larger than others), you may need to wait for up to two minutes for the report to be delivered. Scroll to the bottom of the page and click on "RIGHT Click Here to Download Report" (http://ssq.gsa .gov/getReport.cfm?name=5nhM3i1a.xls) when it appears. The Excel spreadsheet will be an alpha sort and will run through all Schedule holders for that Schedule for the FY selected.

When I am doing research, I usually run reports going back a couple years to see who is growing GSA market share, who is losing GSA market share, and if there are any new players that I need to watch. This multiyear perspective always gives me more detailed information to share with the company for which I am doing the research.

Note that I said GSA market share, not government market share. This is because the GSA is *only one way* the government buys. Those growing or shrinking on the GSA may be using other contracts, and most of the other contracts are not as easy to follow as the GSA. This is especially true for contracts involving higher-end products and services—contracts such as the National Aeronautics and Space Administration Solutions for Enterprise-Wide Procurement (NASA SEWP IV). If you want information on what other contracts a particular company is using, go to the company Web site and look at their press releases. If they are public companies, look at their annual reports. Most companies list all of their government contracts on their Web sites so that government employees visiting the site know how best to access the product or service.

I can predict a couple things for any SSQ report you run for a specific Schedule. The top 5 percent of vendors on each Schedule will take at least 50 percent of the total dollars for that Schedule—sometimes as much as 65 percent. The middle tier, about 30 percent, will take 30 to 40 percent, and the bottom 65 percent of Schedule holders will take less than 10 percent of the dollars, many making zero dollars from the Schedule. I will explain why in Chapter 2.

The GSA sales are a pretty reliable barometer to determine who the players are and where they fit as far as sales go. Make the SSQ part of your government arsenal. This provides you a baseline on the food chain for your niche.

As I have already mentioned, I use both Penton's GovPro and Onvia for research. Both Web sites are content rich, but you will have to pay for some custom research from Onvia. I am not certain whether GovPro performs customer research unless you advertise in their publications.

YOUR TO-DO LIST

1. Understand and accept that there are no "near-term" wins for the novice company in this market. Give yourself 18 to 24 months for a successful market entry.
2. Make no decisions based on one seminar, one book, or one source. Deciding you need a GSA Schedule and getting it may be a mistake. Make decisions slowly, as you will have to live with them for a long time.

3. Determine which information resources are best for your niche. Use each regularly, and share the information internally.

4. Run the SSQ for your niche.

5. Start making a glossary of the terms used in the government market for your niche.

6. Regularly check Web sites such as Acquisition Central for news of changes in the federal acquisition process (https://www.acquisition.gov). This and other valuable links can be found in Appendix 2.

7. Read over the Federal Acquisition Regulations (FAR), Part 9, Contractor Qualifications, available at http://www.terafuel.com/content/gov/far/FARTOCP09.html.

8. Seek advice from qualified professionals. Check out each consultant carefully, including multiple references, before using them.

9. The updated reference guide for this book—the resources and people I recommend—will be available online at www.GovernmentMarketMaster.com.

CHAPTER 2

How the Government Buys

Government purchasing regulations are complex, written in gov-speak, and often require a lawyer for practical translation. Mike Tucker is president of the George W. Allen Company, an office-supply dealer selling to the government market. When he addresses those in his GoverNet group about selling to the government, he always starts with this statement: "The Lord's Prayer contains 56 words; the Gettysburg Address, 266 words; the Ten Commandments, 297 words; the preamble to the Declaration of Independence, 300 words. The U.S. government specification describing a chocolate chip cookie contains 25,600 words."

In an interview I conducted with government sales master Max Peterson, in reference to the "red tape" involved in the government contracting process, Max said, "Where there's mystery, there's margin." The red tape referred to by Max is the myriad of regulations involved in selling to the government. When he says, "Where there's mystery, there's margin," he is simply stating that the better you understand the process, the more likely it is you will be among the winners.

Keep in mind that what I am providing here is a true tip of the iceberg. Be prepared to spend a fair amount of time learning about all this. The Web links provided at the end of this (and every) chapter will help with your ongoing education.

The U.S. federal government is the largest single buyer of goods and services anywhere. The "discretionary" spending will approach $700 billion. Add in state and local government spending and we are dealing in *trillions*.

How the government buys is not unlike peeling an onion: There are always more layers. There are standard ways it buys, and with each layer, there is a sublayer, nuances, and variations. And as Max implied, the more you know about the layers, the more you know about the process, and the more you can make the process work to your advantage.

The red tape Max was talking about centers around the Federal Acquisition Regulations (the FAR). These are the standardized buying procedures and rules for the federal government.

But wait—there's more! Many large federal agencies often have their own supplemental regulations. For example, the Department of Defense has the D-FAR. No wonder there are so many consulting specialists around Washington, DC. Until you learn your way around, you might hire a consultant or lawyer just to translate for you.

The FAR outlines the contracting methods generally employed by federal agencies, including micropurchases, simplified procedures, sealed bidding, contract negotiations, and consolidated purchasing programs.

Let's complicate the matter further. To improve the ability of agencies to purchase goods and services, in 2001, the *President's Management Agenda* outlined 12 initiatives designed to make the government more productive. Shortly thereafter, the Office of Management and Budget (OMB) developed "lines of business" (LOBs). These LOBs were created to consolidate duplicate programs in the federal agencies and to allow agencies to share programs that work well. The intent of the LOBs is to consolidate the "back office" (information technology [IT] and e-government activities) and to integrate programs in order to make overall government operations more efficient and to spend less money. There were originally five lines of business outlined, and there are now nine:

1. Case Management (lead agency is the Department of Justice)
2. Grants Management (lead agencies are Health and Human Services and the National Science Foundation)
3. Health (lead agency is Health and Human Services)
4. Human Resources Management (lead agency is the Office of Personnel Management)
5. Financial Management (lead agency is the GSA)
6. Information Systems Security (no lead agency)
7. Budget Formulation and Execution (lead agency is the OMB with the Education Department)
8. Geospatial (lead agency is the OMB with the Interior Department)
9. IT Infrastructure (lead agency is the OMB with the GSA)

The LOBs are designed to integrate common IT and e-gov–related practices across all agencies into a single standard. This is supposed to save money and reduce the number of FTEs involved in systems that are duplicated throughout government. Steps involved in the transition from legacy systems are determining the parts of the legacy system that should be saved, which parts should be jettisoned, and that which can be salvaged; deciding how to make the transition and pay for it; and determining which contractors can play roles.

While LOBs may not play a direct role in your work, it is another piece of the puzzle you need to be aware of; one of those market nuances that is constantly in flux.

THE MECHANICS OF PURCHASING

Micropurchases: At the low end of the purchasing pyramid, the simplest way the government buys is through credit cards, just like the Visa or MasterCard in your wallet. At the federal level, starting in 1989, the International Merchant Purchase Authorization Card (IMPAC) was the first small purchase card. In 1999, the U.S. General Services Administration issued a new contract for the new SmartPay card. Four banks now issue small purchase government credit cards to about 270,000 federal employees. These cardholders make about 25 million purchases each year via the SmartPay card.

If your average sale is under $3,000, you can do business with the government without contracts.

The credit card was a new way for feds to purchase. Prior to 1989, federal offices used petty cash, called imprest funds. An employee signed for the cash and brought back a receipt. It was an accounting nightmare. In 1989, and for a long while after, a "micropurchase" was any purchase below $2,500, and these purchases *did not require a contract*. The credit card was designed for frontline managers and those with other immediate needs to be able to purchase items quickly, as long as they were purchased from a reliable source and at a competitive price. Again, as no contract was necessary, if you were with the U.S. Army Corps of Engineers and needed some building materials ASAP, you could simply go to a local hardware store and buy what you needed.

In the first year the program was available on a government-wide basis (1989), about $9 million was spent. It has grown considerably since then.

With the SmartPay card, there are no bidding requirements, and there is no competition. The federal employee using the card is supposed to use his or her discretion and buy what is needed at a reasonable price from a reputable dealer.

This was a gold mine for business-to-business (B2B) catalogers and others who sold B2B products and were set up to deliver quickly and process credit card orders. Throughout the 1990s, many direct marketers simply included the IMPAC logo on their catalogs to show that they were "government friendly." Overall, that logo helped create a niche market for those knowledgeable enough to add the IMPAC logo to their promotional materials and Web sites. Without the necessity and headache of managing a government contract, some of the more savvy firms were making several hundred thousands, even millions, each year.

In the last few years, the micropurchase threshold has risen to $3,000, and the SmartPay program processed about $20 billion in small purchases for federal fiscal year (FY) 2009. Purchases under $3,000 still require no contract.

The GSA, which manages the SmartPay program, also manages the fleet card and the travel card under the same program. The fleet card is used for fleet maintenance, gas, and the like. The travel card is used when a federal employee travels and is for travel-related expenses. The entire SmartPay program totaled about $30 billion in FY 2009.

The only time the government credit card program makes the news is when someone misuses a credit card. These are rare occurrences and get much more media play than they should. In fact, the SmartPay program saves the government billions each year by avoiding paper-based procurements (time intensive) for 25 million small purchases. On top of that, agencies get rebates from the issuing banks based on the volume of purchases. The SmartPay program is a good example of a great government program.

GSA SCHEDULES

The best known government contract by far is the GSA Schedule (also known as having a "GSA number"). It is an indefinite-delivery, indefinite-quantity (IDIQ) contract, which means it is open for anyone to buy from, but no one is required to use it. It is a five-year contract, with three five-year renewal options. In effect, having a GSA Schedule is like having a hunting license that allows you to pursue federal business, but it does not make the phone ring.

The phrase "commercial off-the-shelf," or COTS, often refers to what you can get on the GSA Schedule. Larry Allen hosts a radio show that airs on Federal News Radio in Washington, DC, named *Off the Shelf*. Larry is president of the Coalition for Government Procurement, a GSA advocacy and educational organization. Tuning in to his show is an excellent way to stay current on some of the issues (www .FederalNewsRadio.com; 1500 AM in Washington, DC).

The GSA Schedules are actually a series of contracts under one name. Each Schedule is a contract for a specific type of product or service, and each has a number or a number and letter combination. Under each Schedule, there are subsets known as special item numbers, or SINs, which further define the product.

The Schedules fall into 43 separate categories. These cover virtually any and all business products and services. All told, over 12 million commercial items are available through the GSA Schedules, and there are over 20,000 contract holders. Some companies hold more than one GSA contract, so it is estimated that there are about 12,000 companies with GSA contracts. The following are examples of GSA Schedules:

- Schedule 36: Office, Imaging and Document Solutions
- Schedule 48: Transportation, Delivery and Relocation Solutions
- Schedule 51 V: Hardware SuperStore
- Schedule 58 I: Professional Audio/Video, Telemetry/ Tracking, Recording/Reproducing, and Signal Data Solutions
- Schedule 67: Photographic Equipment—Cameras, Photographic Printers, and Related Supplies and Services
- Schedule 70: General Purpose Commercial Information Technology Equipment, Software and Services
- Schedule 71: Furniture

- Schedule 874: Mission Oriented Business Integrated Services (MOBIS), which now includes the older Schedule 69: Training Aids and Devices—Instructor-Led Training, Course Development, and Test Administration

The GSA Schedules are popular for both vendors and agency buyers because they represent preapproved products and services at prices that have been negotiated on behalf of the federal government.

There are some caveats for those considering getting a GSA Schedule as the entry point of doing business with Uncle Sam:

- The Schedule does not guarantee you business. It is a contract from which you can sell, so be proactive.

- The GSA gets a 0.75 percent rebate on all sales through your Schedule(s) on a quarterly basis. This is the Industrial Funding Fee (IFF).

- You are subject to audits by the GSA to ensure you are paying your IFF.

- You have to produce at least $25,000 in annual activity on your GSA by year two of your first five years in order to stay on the Schedule.

- Selling from a GSA Schedule requires different skills than normal B2B sales.

- The more you learn about the Schedule, the more valuable it can become for you.

While over one-third of government procurement transactions occur through the GSA Schedules, less than 10 percent of the dollars spent by the federal government are spent through the program. In FY 2009, $37.5 billion were spent through the GSA Schedules. So, while popular, the GSA represents the tip of the iceberg on federal spending.

OTHER CONTRACTING METHODS

When the government wants to purchase a product or service, it has multiple methods at its disposal. It may choose an
existing contract, such as the GSA Schedule or a task order on
another contract, or it may opt to look elsewhere. This largely
depends on the dollar size of the purchase and the current
workload of the procurement office.

Micropurchases: As already discussed and as defined in the
government market (FAR and the Service Contract Act), a
micropurchase is any purchase under $3,000. These purchases
can be made with a government small purchase credit card
(SmartPay), and they may be made from any legitimate vendor
for a product or service required by a federal employee in the
execution of his or her job. These purchases do not have to be
advertised or competed. No contract is required when making
micropurchases, so a government employee with a credit card
may walk into a local hardware store and make a purchase with
the card, as long as what he or she is buying is necessary in his
or her job. That same employee may be at a small regional office
with no convenient store nearby, in which case the employee
may opt to purchase from a catalog that offers the needed
product and guarantees delivery in an acceptable time frame.

The normal credit card per-purchase limit is $3,000,
although there are a small percentage of the cards that have a
higher per-purchase level. These are warrant cards, and some
of these have per-purchase levels well into five figures.

The purchase limits on all SmartPay cards are subject to
"extreme conditions." Under extreme conditions, generally
defined as times of national emergency, the card threshold goes
up to $15,000 inside the United States and $25,000 outside the
country (OCONUS).

Simplified acquisition procedures (SAP) apply to purchases
over $3,000 and under $100,000. Purchases under $100,000
require less administrative hassle for the buyer, lower approval
levels, and less overall documentation. If the purchase is under

$25,000, it can be made by obtaining (and documenting) oral or written quotes. These purchases under $25,000 do not have to be advertised. Any planned purchase above $25,000 requires posting at the Federal Business Opportunities (FBO) Web site, available at www.fbo.gov. All purchases under $100,000 are *supposed* to be reserved for small businesses. The caveat here is that if a contracting officer cannot find two small businesses that qualify on price, quality, or delivery, the contract can go to any qualified bidder. This is also known as "the rule of two" and is a hotly disputed topic with small business activists. Details on simplified acquisition are in FAR, Part 13.

Sealed bidding (also known as *formal advertising*) is when the government issues *invitations for bid* (IFB). The product or service sought is carefully defined, as are all other requirements, which include instructions on preparing the bid, as not all IFBs are the same. Other instructions will include conditions for the purchase, packaging, delivery, shipping and payment, any other contract clauses determined to be necessary, and a due date for the bid.

The bids are opened in public, usually in the office that issued the IFB, and any bidder may attend. The award is usually based on price and other price-related factors; especially important is meeting all established criteria defined in the bid. The most responsive low bidder wins. Some companies will get an IFB directly—especially those companies the agency is familiar with and thinks can do the job. For others, IFBs and links to them are posted at www.fbo.gov. Sealed bidding regulations are defined in FAR, Part 14.

Contract negotiations can and probably will occur whenever the value of a government contract exceeds $100,000 or when the product or service being acquired is extremely technical. Products and services that are more off-the-shelf could be purchased through the GSA Schedule, but when more technical solutions are needed, the government may issue a *request for proposal* (RFP). A typical RFP outlines the requirement in detail; then, the issuing office solicits proposals

from prospective contractors. These will appear at www.fbo
.com. The responders indicate how they intend to deliver the
requested product or service and at what price. Proposals
are often subject to negotiation after they have been submitted.

When the government has a possible requirement and
wants to know what is available, it may issue a *request for quo-
tation* (RFQ) outlining the product or service sought. Any
response to an RFQ by a prospective contractor isn't considered
an offer and cannot be accepted by the government to form a
binding contract. It is simply a potential quote. Government-
wide RFPs and RFQs and links to them are available at www
.fbo.gov. Again, those with a history of providing the agency
with quality products and services may get the RFP directly.

Government contracting goes though a regular (some say predictable) pendulum effect, often driven by the whims of someone in Congress or a new administration. One of the more recent
pendulum swings in federal acquisition policy is the increased
importance of "best value." Rather than simply awarding to the
lowest bidder, as often happened in the past, the government can
now make awards for the product or service based on a defined
best value at a somewhat premium price. To do so, the agency
must clearly state its intent to use best value criteria in the solicitation. The solicitation must then include a detailed description of
the evaluation criteria, award factors, and any factors other than
price that will be considered in making the award. The weight for
each criterion is also supposed to be stated.

Best value often occurs when a good business development professional has been working in an agency, understands
its mission and other issues, and thinks his or her company or
a specific technology may best suit the clients' needs. That
person supplies sufficient information to those in the agency
involved in determining the scope of work required. If the
agency personnel agree that a specific solution will help fulfill a
requirement, it can influence the RFP. We will discuss the role
of business development in more detail in Chapter 5.

Another recent trend is the focus on past performance. This heavily favors companies with a long and successful track record in the market. It is designed to give vendors a rating for each contract they have previously worked on, giving the contracting officer a level of comfort regarding the work they need accomplished.

As these larger contracts are usually awarded to larger companies, part of the contract may require a small business subcontracting plan. This will outline when and how the large contractor will use small businesses during the course of the contract. For small businesses, this means reading the contract specifications carefully and identifying areas where your technical strength may be an asset to a prime contractor bidding for that business.

Contract negotiations are discussed in detail in FAR, Part 15.

Consolidated purchasing programs: Most government agencies have similar purchasing needs for the types of products or services purchased, such as office supplies, furniture, facilities maintenance, and training. Sometimes, the government can achieve economies of scale by centralizing the purchasing of these products and services.

The government may use "acquisition vehicles," such as multiagency contracts and GWACs, to encourage long-term vendor agreements with fewer suppliers. The use of these acquisition vehicles (also called multiple award contracts, or MACs) has increased over the last few years but has recently faced some scrutiny from the current administration. The MAC contracts allow federal buyers to quickly fill requirements by placing orders against existing contracts without starting a new procurement action from scratch. Agencies can also award multiple "task order" contracts (which involve indefinite delivery and indefinite quantity) to allow more than one firm to deliver a particular product or service.

Details on the types of contracts are found in FAR, Part 16.

SET-ASIDE PROCUREMENTS

When the government feels small businesses can fulfill a government need, they will create a set-aside contract. Other contracts may be awarded to both large and small contractors. In
those contracts where a portion is not directly open to small
business, there is usually a subcontracting provision requiring
any winning contractor to have a small business utilization
plan as part of their proposal. The small business subcontracting plan is required from large businesses, when the work is
performed in the United States, and must be approved by the
agency awarding the contract prior to the award. The contractor must include small business goals for the contract and also
designate a small business liaison officer (SBLO).

After a determination is made that a contract can be a
set-aside contract, the government first looks at historically
underutilized business zone (HUBZone) companies, then
service-disabled veteran-owned small businesses (SDVOSBs),
and then 8(a)s, firms owned and operated by socially and
economically disadvantaged individuals and eligible to receive
federal contracts under the Small Business Administration's
(SBA) 8(a) Business Development Program.

To make the determination of whether a contract is viable
for set-aside, the government issues market research notices
called *requests for information* (RFIs), also called "sources sought
notices." These can come out when the government is looking
for information on if and how to set aside a potential contract.
If they get enough interest from small businesses, then they
can set it aside. If they don't, then it's usually a full and open
(unrestricted) procurement. The information the government
receives helps determine how they will make the procurement.

Many companies don't respond to RFIs because there is no
work directly attached to them; it is viewed as spinning tires.
If small businesses do not respond to the RFIs, it may open the
way for larger companies to bid, when it could have been a
set-aside contract.

There are online and offline ways to monitor current and emerging set-aside programs. You can certainly monitor set-asides through www.fbo.com, and that should be part of your weekly reading. Other free and online services include DefenseLink (www.defenselink.mil/contracts), which posts information on military and defense contracts starting at $5 million, and the SBA SUB-Net registry (http://web.sba.gov/subnet). Many of the services available through the government have e-news alerts that you can sign up to receive.

In addition, each federal agency has a small business information page. Updated resources are listed at www.Government MarketMaster.com. Click on the book cover and the updated resources mentioned in this book will be there.

One of the paid services I use is *Set-Aside Alert* (www .setasidealert.com). This publication has been around since 1992, and the service provides a daily e-mail update and a biweekly newsletter. The articles and interviews are always informative. Paid services such as this one usually add a dose of reality to the mix. While the government-issued information is pretty good, it shows none of the warts of the market. The interviews in publications like *Set-Aside Alert* provide a somewhat clearer picture.

I have mentioned the FBO several times. The Federal Business Opportunities Web site (www.fbo.gov) can be a good place to do research and familiarize yourself with not only what the government buys but also how it buys—especially how it buys your product or service. All purchases over $25,000 are supposed to be reported here—Department of Defense (DoD) and civilian. I suggest you take the tutorial, accessed by clicking the "Getting Started" button on the top navigation bar.

At the FBO Web site, you can search for active contracts or archived contracts by type of notice; by the solicitation or award number; by the place of performance (zip code); by set-aside type; by North American Industry Classification System (NAICS) codes, federal supply codes (FSC), or product service codes (PSC); by keywords; or by agency. While there, you should register to receive all notices for your NAICS, FSC, and PSC.

Competition requirements are discussed at length in FAR, Part 6. These include *full and open competition*, where all responsible sources are permitted to compete; *full and open competition after exclusion of sources*, where it can be determined which companies may compete; and *other than full and open competition*, where the agency may use a sole source provider or where there are extenuating circumstances such as "urgency," industrial mobilization, international agreement, actions authorized or required by statute, or national security.

THE REALITY OF PURCHASING

In my interviews with Max Peterson, he said that the trick is not simply offering contracts that are attractive to your customer but creating buying vehicles that are available to the customer and that are unique, or nearly so, to your company.

The more you and your frontline staff learn about selling from a Schedule, or any GWAC/IDIQ contract, the better off you'll be. There are a variety of ways to do this, and we will only touch on a few, especially as they pertain to the GSA Schedule.

If you are selling from a GSA Schedule and you identify a specific opportunity and want to get the customer to buy quickly, you can offer a *spot reduction* from your Schedule price. This method is employed when you identify a need, but the customer is really limited in how much can be spent. If you can retain some margin and/or build a stronger relationship with this buyer, this method may help. A spot reduction must be documented properly, but in effect, it allows you to offer a one-time price reduction to a specific customer for a specific purchase. This will result in a sale, but it has to be documented for and reported to your GSA account representative.

If it looks like it may be a longer-term opportunity for a specific product, a *blanket purchase agreement* (BPA) may be an answer. A BPA defines a time period and products available to a specific agency (one agency, not all) and offers a price reduction based on the potential of the deal. It is not mandatory that an agency use a BPA, so be as certain as you can before setting them up that they will pay dividends.

Task orders are another contract subset. When a government customer has a specific need, they may decide to use a task order. The paperwork involved is less onerous than going after a separate contract, but it will involve a document that includes a task description, the scope of the work, and an agreed-upon price. There is always controversy surrounding the use of task orders—even protests—but they continue to be popular with overworked government contracting officers.

We will be discussing the reality of leveraging contracts throughout this book. The more you know, the better off you will be.

YOUR TO-DO LIST

1. Maintain ongoing education for C-level and key staff.
2. Designate one staffer as the point person to learn everything possible about contracting. Provide that person with all the support necessary. Memberships in the National Contract Management Association and/or the Association of Proposal Management Professionals would be good.
3. Attend contract briefings at federal agencies.
4. Check in at www.GovernmentMarketMaster.com for events.
5. Add these Web sites to those you visit:
   www.govexec.com/basics
   www.acquisition.gov/Far/90-37/html/toc.html
   www.acq.osd.mil/osbp/doing_business/index.htm

CHAPTER 3

Determining Where You Fit

Prime Contractor, Subcontractor, GSA Schedule, Open Market, or All of the Above

Primes, subs, Schedules—oh my! Like Dorothy in the Land of Oz, there is a lot of potentially confusing information when determining where and how you fit in the government contracting landscape.

There are different paths for different companies. Companies that sell products use a different path than those that sell services. Those selling true commodity products will have different options than those selling higher-end products. Those that sell lower-end less technical services may take a different path than those selling higher-end services. If you qualify as a small business by the Small Business Administration (SBA) standards, you may have further options.

There are four major paths to take when doing business with the government: open market vendor, prime contractor, subcontractor, or GSA Schedule sales. Most successful contractors take more than one path.

One size does not fit all, even for two companies selling the same thing. So, before you proceed, answer these questions: Are you a product vendor? If so, is it a commodity product or a higher-end product? If you are a service vendor, the same applies. Be honest with yourself. The more realistic you are, the more likely it is you will succeed.

Many companies enter the government market because they have heard or read something that indicated they could make money there. There have been hundreds if not thousands of articles on the stimulus program alone that drove thousands of companies to visit government and nongovernment Web sites, looking for the stimulus money the government was allegedly handing out. Many of these companies expected to enter and make money in a short period of time. Much of this information was misguided, some perhaps intentionally.

Those companies that fall for the "easy path to government contract" nonsense that is out there are doomed. Companies entering the government market with high expectations of quick money often end up as chalk outlines on the sidewalk. There are no quick hits in this market.

Before we go any further, let's make one thing very clear: Any time you hear something about the government market that seems too good to be true, understand that it probably is too good to be true. Check the credentials of any and all information providers you use. Google is a wonderful tool for this. If you find anything questionable about the information source, the easiest thing to do is move on. There are lots of good sources of information and lots of excellent consultants in this market. Don't waste your time on any consultant where they may be some doubt.

Anything you are trying to get started in the government market requires lots of time. The government never moves at your pace.

WORKING WITH THE GOVERNMENT IS DIFFERENT!

Once your company has made a determination regarding doing business with the government, the next question is how. Here is how one company really got a good start. The following story is from Dendy Young, former chief executive officer (CEO) of Falcon Microsystems and GTSI. He is now chairman of McLean Capital.

> I remember when Apple first delivered their vision for consumer-based computing, the Lisa, allegedly named for Steve Jobs's then girlfriend. The Lisa, with its mouse, graphical screen icons, and WYSIWYG ("what you see is what you get") printer, pioneered the expectations of later generations of computer users, who today, whether they use Windows 7, RedHat Unix, Ubuntu, Apple Snow Leopard, or the iPhone, all take the Lisa's breakthroughs as a given standard.
>
> Apple Computer, having been started by a couple of college dropouts in a garage, knew little about the size or sophistication of government business. They didn't realize that to do business with the federal government required focus and dedication, just like it does to do business with any class or group of customers. In fact, Steve Jobs, in the context of the post-Vietnam era, is quoted as saying, "We don't want to do business with the government because they make bombs and kill people!"
>
> So, when government agencies wanted to buy Macs, they had a hard time doing so—in particular, the agencies were not used to buying from storefronts: They wanted professional sales and support organizations to deal with.
>
> My company, Falcon Microsystems, approached Apple with the proposition that we could "protect and shield" Apple from the vagaries and complexities of the government market. With great reluctance, because

it seemed like a violation of their ethics, they agreed to go ahead.

So, Falcon put Apple products on GSA Schedule and began to gain additional contracts for Apple. We demonstrated the product tirelessly at every tabletop show and event. A number of third-party manufacturers grew up providing products that filled the "holes" in the Apple product line: When customers wanted a larger or a smaller monitor that Apple refused to provide, third parties like Radius would step in, and together, we would exceed our customers' expectations. We bundled the product with compatible third-party products, both hardware and software, thereby creating integrated solutions for our customers. We sold thousands of "presentation systems" to our DoD customers, who reveled in the elegant output of the Tektronix solid-ink printers for their presentation slides. We provided help-desk, hardware maintenance, and engineering support for our customers.

Despite Apple's unresponsiveness to the government customer, we built a company that was dedicated to Apple that sold hundreds of millions of dollars of Apple-based solutions to the federal government.

In the early 1990s, Apple concluded that they would be able to sell more to the federal government if they had a lot more dealers than just Falcon, so they broadened their distribution channel to many other dealers. Shortly thereafter, Falcon was sold to GTSI Corp, and Apple's market share in government declined markedly.

The moral of the story is this:

1. When entering the government market, you are better off working with an organization that focuses and concentrates on government business.

2. Whatever your internal culture may be, you should realize that commercial cultures and government-oriented cultures are impossible to mix successfully—unless you have critical mass.
3. As a commercial company, in order to sell your product or service to the government, you must either work through a third party that already knows the government or you must build up sufficient critical mass so that the two different cultures can coexist within the same company.
4. One solution is to work through a government-centric company until you reach sufficient revenues to justify your own government division with the ability to develop and support your government customers.

Dendy was a master of the reseller scene from the 1980s until he left GTSI in 2007. I advised him and his marketing people at both Falcon Microsystems and GTSI and learned a great deal during my time with each.

The *reseller role* is well illustrated in this story. Regardless of Mr. Jobs's reasons for not wanting to deal directly with the government, it was a smart move. Most manufacturers will be much better served dealing with the "channel" to sell to the government than going direct. When you sell direct, you need your own contracts and your own sales force; you must build an infrastructure that may not fit your core business at all.

Resellers in the government market sell all types of products to the government, from the low-end pure commodity products through the high-end information technology (IT) and mechanical and scientific instruments. Manufacturers use the channel because if you select the right reseller, you get profits from the government without the maintenance hassles associated with the sales and contracting process. The resellers carry GSA Schedules, BPAs, and other GWACs that provide a vehicle for commodity products. The reseller can append new manufacturers to existing contracts.

If you are a manufacturer looking at the government market, carefully consider coming in through the resellers. While they may ask for training, sales assistance, and funding for marketing, it is still a much saner way to enter the market.

GSA SALES AND THE SSQ

The next step is researching your niche to determine the size of the market for whatever you sell. I often refer to this as figuring out where you are in the food chain. If your focus is federal, the best place to start the research is the GSA Schedule. The GSA Schedule sales are a great barometer, but in fact, the GSA Schedule represents less than 10 percent of federal spending. It remains, however, a great place for determining who the competition is and where they rank in sales for each category. While the information you get only pertains to GSA sales, you start to see who the dominant players are.

Using the SSQ tool, you can start your quest. This is a great tool, and it is important that you learn how to use it. The SSQ (http://ssq.gsa.gov) allows you to see the sales reported by our Federal Supply Schedule contractors themselves. These are not final or official figures, but they are close. The SSQ report generator lets you select a preformatted report for the information you are looking for based on a specific Schedule, time frame (up to five years back), and SIN. The GSA built this system based on recurrent requests for specific information. There are 11 reports from which to choose, available as text for download, text for printing, or an Excel spreadsheet. The report options are as follows:

1. All Schedules by fiscal year (each FY separately)
2. All Schedules by all available fiscal years (five FYs on one report)
3. SIN and Schedule totals by fiscal year
4. All contract sales by Schedule by fiscal year
5. Schedule sales grand total by quarter by fiscal year
6. Total for all quarters by contractor by fiscal year
7. Total by quarter and SIN by contract number and fiscal year
8. Total for each quarter for a specific SIN by fiscal year

9. Total by quarter and contract for a specific contractor and fiscal year

10. Total by contractor for a specific Schedule and fiscal year

11. All sales by fiscal year for a specific SIN number

Using this tool, you can find out the total spend for each GSA Schedule, get a list of all companies on each Schedule, and see how much they made for a specific time period, in an entire fiscal year, or by quarter. I use the tenth option, total by contractor for a specific Schedule and fiscal year, when I am doing initial research for most clients.

For example, when doing research for an office-supply company recently, I used the SSQ to run a report on Schedule 75. I was quickly able to see that for FY 2009, Schedule 75 had 536 contractors and a total spend of $691,655,653. If this were a level playing field and you divided this up between the 536 contractors, each would receive about $1,301, 596.

But it doesn't work that way. The top five Schedule 75 contractors (ABM Federal, Office Depot, Office Max, Staples, and Industries for the Blind) took $252 million, approximately 35 percent of the dollars awarded in FY 2009. Forty-four companies made zero dollars, and another 95 made under $25,000. That's a total of 139 companies receiving under $25,000 — more than 25 percent of the contractors. The $25,000 mark is important, because the GSA gives you a two-year window to grow your sales to at least that amount before they have the option to take the Schedule away from you. It is in their best interest to have companies on the Schedule that are producing.

Now you have your first handle on the GSA, and that's good, because it's what we're discussing next.

YOUR ROLE(S): GSA, OPEN MARKET, PRIME, OR SUB?

For those pursuing direct relations with the government, at the low end for products and services, the GSA Schedule is a viable option. This can be an attractive option if you are willing to learn how to use the Schedule to your advantage. The GSA Schedule will also be attractive for higher-end products and services as well, as would GWAC contracts such as the NASA SEWP.

There is an old baseball saying, "You can't tell the players without a scorecard." Selling from a GSA Schedule requires several things, not the least of which include the following:

- Knowing which agencies need what you sell
- Knowing who in those agencies are influencers and who are buyers
- Knowing how to reach them
- Understanding the budget cycle, especially knowing if end of FY will impact your sales

And the list goes on.

If you average order is under $3,000 and you really don't want to pursue contracts, you can try to build your business through *open market* (noncontract) sales by going after the SmartPay cardholders. The best methods for reaching the government credit card holders are mailing directly to them (a mailing list of over 150,000 SmartPay cardholders is available from MeritDirect), including the SmartPay logo on your Web site, and using your collateral material.

Prime contractors are companies that bid directly on government contracts. The skills required to prime, except on very small bids, will be beyond the capabilities of novice companies and beyond many except the most skilled small businesses. Competition for government work that goes to bid is always intense and requires dedicated personnel (in-house or consultants) to work on and monitor the bid until award. I strongly urge novices not to attempt this route. There are better ways— smaller steps to take first.

Bob Davis has a list of 18 criteria that primes look for when considering subcontractors. Here are a few:

- What value do our customers receive from the sub's product(s)?
- Does the firm have a real strategic plan? What is the three-year vision?
- What are the firm's *truly unique* skills and assets?
- What is the nature and sophistication of the firm's marketing assets (e.g., industry and marketing research, environmental scanning, brand management, pricing analyses, and competitive analyses)?
- What are the firm's strengths, discriminators, and sustainable competitive advantages?
- How is "quality" executed in the firm?
- Who is responsible for generation of new business?

If you want to get on the radar of a prime contractor, you need to be aware of everything they are looking for, not just your core strength. The list will always include financial stability. The primes are always on the lookout for a great small business partner, one that can fill in any technical areas in which they may require help, but you have to meet all the requirements, not just the technical criteria.

Okay, so maybe you are not going to prime—at least not right away. How, then, can you identify some *subcontracting* opportunities? The first thing to do is get educated on what is required. Procurement technical assistance centers (PTACs), small business development centers (SBDCs), and the Service Corps of Retired Executives (SCORE) volunteers can all be starting places for this education, but it has to continue into the agency or agencies you wish to target, through the Office of Small and Disadvantaged Business Utilization (OSDBU), through identifying contractors who have a history with the agencies in question, and more, as always.

The PTACs and SBDCs can help you understand the process of subcontracting, but it comes down to a few basics:

- Define what you do really well (your differentiator, your competitive advantage—whatever you want to call it, but be specific). Your major skill is always your first message.
- Identify the agencies that may need this skill.
- Identify the contractors that work with the agency.
- Identify the contracts in place that call for this skill.
- Find ways to get to key agency personnel to tell them what you do, and find ways to get in front of the contractors with the same message.

If you do not lead with your strength, here is what will happen: nothing. Other things that will put you on the radar of the contractor could include the following:

- A highly sought-after skill or area of expertise
- Some agency relationships
- Some good press, preferably recent
- Knowledge of the people inside the prime contract company

Another way to get in front of prime contractors is through their small business outreach offices. Many prime contractors have people responsible for this, and you can see them at various industry functions—most notably at events such as the annual OSDBU conference and other agency-specific small business events. The day I was writing this, I received an announcement for the small business outreach conference for the Social Security Administration in Baltimore.

Among the reasons to attend these events is to meet the agency small business personnel and to set appointments but also to meet the small business outreach people from the prime contractors. Among others, I always see General Dynamics IT at most of these events. Their small business liaison professional is Ludmilla Parnell, and she is quite active at these events.

I keep mentioning the small business side of things, so let's see where you fit.

SIZE MATTERS

Let's deal with small business size status. To determine whether you qualify as a small business, take a look at the SBA size standards at www.sba.gov. The SBA size standards for small businesses are determined by the NAICS code. The standards vary by business category.

If you are a legitimate small business, you need to make the best determination as to which small business category you fit into. The following text lists the categories as defined by the SBA and FAR. These are directly from the SBA Web site, with minor additions and clarification by me. Details can be found in FAR, Parts 19 and 26.

Small business (SB): Located in the United States; organized for profit; independently owned and operated, including affiliates; not dominant in field of operations in which it is bidding on government contracts; *and* meets the SBA size standards included in solicitation. Size standard is based upon the NAICS assigned to the specific procurement dependent upon the product and/or service purchased. Small businesses are self-certified.

Woman-owned small business (WOSB): Small business; at least 51 percent owned by one or more women; *and* management and daily business operations controlled by one or more women. Woman-owned business status is self-certified.

Small disadvantaged business (SDB): Small business; unconditionally owned and controlled by one or more socially and economically disadvantaged individuals who are of good character and are citizens of the United States; *and* SBA certified. Small disadvantaged businesses are certified by the SBA.

Small disadvantaged business 8(a) certified (also simply called an 8[a]): Small business; SBA certified as an SDB; *and* SBA certified into the 8(a) Business Development Program for a period of nine years. The 8(a)s are certified by the SBA.

Historically underutilized business zone (HUBZone): Small business; at least 51 percent owned and controlled by U.S. citizens; and SBA certified as a HUBZone concern (principal office located in a designated HUBZone and at least 35 percent of employees live in a HUBZone). Historically underutilized business zones are certified by the SBA.

Veteran-owned small business (VOSB): Small business; veteran owned as defined in 38 United States Code (USC) 101(2); at least 51 percent owned by one or more veterans; and management and/or daily operations controlled by one or more veterans. Veteran-owned small businesses are self-certified.

Service-disabled veteran-owned small business (SDVOSB): Small business; veteran owned; at least 51 percent owned by one or more service-disabled veterans; *and* management and daily business operations controlled by one or more service-disabled veterans *or* in the case of veteran with permanent and severe disability, the spouse or permanent caregiver of such veteran; *and* with zero to 100 percent service-connected disability as defined in 38 USC 101(16) and as documented on the Defense Department Form 214 or equivalent. Service-disabled veteran-owned small businesses are self-certified.

Now that you know what your business status is, we migrate to establishing your credentials. On the pure mechanics side, the first step is registering your business in the Central Contractor Registration (CCR) system, available at www.ccr.gov. While you may want to farm out this work or let someone else in your organization handle it, it is important that you know how it is done and that you verify some of the information yourself. After all, you probably know your company better than anyone else, right?

ESTABLISHING THE COMPANY CREDENTIALS

As we mentioned before, the government is regulation intense. The various identification classifications and codes required in the government market are as important for a contractor as social security numbers are for individuals. Having a detailed knowledge of your products and services is important, but it's more important to be able to quickly and clearly communicate that information to government agencies. The government people will be looking up SINs and product service codes (PSCs), not "executive office chair." They identify these products and services in very different ways than you and me.

The people reviewing your bid or proposal may be reviewing multiple submissions, and they will be looking for certain identification codes to make a determination as to whether your business is a good fit. If they don't find what they are looking for in the exact place it is supposed to be, your proposal is placed in the "not qualified" pile.

Government request for proposals (RFPs) require gov-speak, including the necessary product and/or service codes such as PSCs or SINs and much more. In most government RFPs, a variety of identification codes are required. Defining your business in the government's terms will also allow you to sign up for contractor registries and buyer-vendor matching services.

So, before you start your registration process, let's get your house in order.

Data Universal Numbering System (DUNS): Dun & Bradstreet's nine-digit DUNS code is a standard business identifier for both the government and the private sector. It is important for several reasons. Since the late 1990s, the federal government has used the DUNS to identify contractors for all procurement-related activities. You probably already have a DUNS number, but you need to check. If you don't have one, register your company ASAP. This puts your company in the Dun & Bradstreet database and will include contact, financial, and industry information that allows other companies and government agencies to check out your credentials. Registering a DUNS number is free. To register your company to pursue government contracts or grants, go to http://fedgov.dnb.com/webform/displayHomePage.do.

NAICS codes: The NAICS codes replaced the old Standard Industrial Classification (SIC) codes several years ago. The NAICS is a system developed by the governments of the United States, Canada, and Mexico to classify business establishments and simplify trade. It is used by federal, state, and local governments to classify potential vendors.

You can find the right NAICS code for your business by going to http://www.census.gov/naics and clicking on "2007 NAICS Search" on the upper left-hand side of the page. Enter keywords related to your business until you find the NAICS code or codes that best fit your business. There will probably be more than one. I suggest you download and browse the complete list of NAICS codes and pick those that suit your core business. Most federal agencies will accept more than one code, and you will find that having multiple NAICS codes may help you in bidding.

The CCR (www.ccr.gov), discussed in the next section, will accept up to 5 or 10 NAICS codes, depending on the business. If you have trouble determining your NAICS code, you may request assistance by clicking on the "Contact Us" button at the bottom of the page.

Federal Supply Classification (FSC): The FSC was developed by the federal government and is mainly used by the DoD. A complete list of FSC codes is available at http://www.drms.dla.mil/asset/fsclist.html.

REGISTERING YOUR COMPANY
WITH THE GOVERNMENT

Now that we have done the fun stuff and your business is properly classified, the next step is to actually register your business so that you can bid. Keep in mind that registration is a process; it does not guarantee you any work. Remember that at the beginning of the book I told you there were over 560,000 companies already registered. Think of the lottery slogan, "You gotta play to win." In this case, you've got to register to play before you can win.

CCR: The first stop of places to register is the CCR. The CCR is used by all federal agencies, and once registered, you can bid on any federal contract for which you qualify. Registering with the CCR places your business information in a centralized vendor database accessible to all federal contracting offices. It is important to keep your CCR information up to date.

To register for the CCR, you need to gather detailed information on your business in several areas. There are some guides (available as pdf files) to CCR available online, including the CCR handbook, which can be found at www.wapa.gov/ business/PDF/CCR_Handbook.pdf. This site details all the information you need, and the CCR frequently asked questions (FAQs) page, available at www.bpn.gov/ccr/FAQ.aspx, will answer all your questions and provide good examples.

You start with your DUNS number; Commercial and Government Entity (CAGE) code; company name; federal tax ID number; business location; receipts; number of employees; Web site address; business type and any applicable SBA-defined small business status; NAICS code; SIC code; PSC; FSC (aren't you glad you know what the acronyms stand for? You're already learning gov-speak!); your bank and American Bankers Association routing number; bank account number; remittance address; lockbox number; automated clearing house information; electronic data interchange information, with point of contact (POC) and their contact information; and business credit card information. And there is more: POC information for the primary contact and alternate POCs, an electronic commerce POC, and a past performance and/or government POC. If necessary, these can be the same person.

While a CAGE code is one of the listed requirements, you don't get one until you register at the CCR. That's a little confusing, but now you know. Registering for the CCR will automatically validate you through the CAGE code system, and you are then assigned a CAGE code. The CAGE code is just another government code used to classify your business.

If you're a small business as defined by SBA regulations, you should complete the "Dynamic Small Business Search" function in the supplemental information section. It is an extra step that can get your business more exposure. Occasionally, federal agencies will use this small business search tool to find contractors that provide precisely what they need.

After you finish the CCR registration, you'll create a Marketing Partner Identification Number, which becomes your password for various other federal government systems, including the Online Representations and Certifications Application.

Online Representations and Certifications Application (ORCA): The ORCA (I love that name!) was developed to reduce the amount of paperwork (!) involved in federal contracting. It actually does reduce the amount of paperwork, too. Most federal RFPs require that you represent and certify various facts regarding your company, including company size, revenue, compliance with pertinent federal regulations, and more. All of these are required. Each RFP is different, but many of the certification elements are the same. With a current ORCA profile, all this is taken care of up front.

While much of the information in CCR and ORCA is the same, the major difference is that ORCA provides the information companies are required to certify to be eligible for government contracts. Regardless of the seemingly duplicative effort, you must register with both CCR and ORCA.

You need your DUNS number and an active registration with the CCR before you can register with ORCA. Once you start the ORCA registration, your CCR data should transfer automatically, so at least you don't have to enter it all over again. After that happens, you will get a several-page questionnaire asking for details about your business. Respond truthfully; this is not a marketing brochure. This is an online certification that you are providing to Uncle Sam so that you can get some of your hard-earned tax dollars back in the form of a government contract. There are penalties associated with not being truthful. For the step-by-step instructions, go to https://orca .bpn.gov/help/help.aspx.

Now, you are almost ready to enter the fray!

YOUR TO-DO LIST

1. Attend some training events organized by PTACs and others. Begin to gain an understanding of what the market entails and where you could fit.
2. Start developing a circle of friends and advisors who can help you along the way.
3. Identify some of the small business conferences in your area. If you are not in DC, many members of Congress host events and bring in speakers.
4. Make a list of the Web sites mentioned and visit them regularly.
5. Develop an internal educational program for your staff on doing business with the government.
6. Depending on the size of your company, dedicate a lead person or team to government dealings.

CHAPTER 4

Infrastructure Issues

What Your Company Needs to Succeed

At the beginning of Chapter 2, I referenced an interview I conducted with Max Peterson, where in reference to government procurement regulations, he said, "Where there's mystery, there's margin." Max was talking from a position of knowledge: If you know the regulations, you can use that knowledge to your advantage when selling, bidding, partnering, subcontracting, and more. Understanding how the government buys also involves knowing what the government expects from the contractors serving the market. Max's ability to sell was in part predicated on his confidence that the infrastructure was in place behind him and his sales force.

To be successful in any business, certain factors and skills have to be in place. Among these are the sales and marketing function, finance and payroll, human resources, legal and security issues, computer systems, management and administration, and something to sell.

This seems pretty straightforward, and when a novice company enters the market, they are usually not thinking about how these key infrastructure issues will need to adapt to a new market. In reality, all but one need to adjust.

To illustrate this point, here's an example.

ALL THAT WORK AND NO PAY . . .

A couple years back, I received a call from a friend of a friend. My friend JoAnna Brandi (also known as the "Customer Care Coach") does lots of public speaking, and she is asked about lots of things, not all of which are germane to her area of expertise. The result was this phone call. I get these calls from time to time, but this one was a little different. The woman calling had spent two years pursuing government business and had finally won a small contract. She had been performing work on the contract, delivering what was required, and doing what she thought she needed to do.

Except her invoices were going unpaid. So, when she complained to JoAnna, she was told I could help, and she called me. In turn, I referred her to Courtney Fairchild of Global Services, Inc. Courtney is an expert in government contracts and GSA Schedules, and she was able to show the novice contractor how to get paid. Instead of the required government paperwork, the contractor had been sending her standard invoices to the government office, and they were ignored. Once the right paperwork was in place, she started getting paid. Problem solved.

Well, let's assume the *first* problem was solved. It is apparent that while this woman was busy pursuing her first contract, she still did not bother to learn about all the other issues that go along with being a government contractor.

This is a simple example—truly the tip of the iceberg for complying with how the government does business. If you don't do it the government's way, things go awry quickly. You need several pieces of the puzzle in place to pursue government business, including specialists in the bid and proposal, legal, and accounting areas. These can be in-house professionals or retainer-based consultants, but proceeding without adult supervision in these areas can lead to big problems. But before you can even begin to get help, you need to know where the potential problem areas are.

INFRASTRUCTURE ISSUES

These are infrastructure issues—things that you have in place for your commercial business but that can be very different when doing business with the government. So, let's go back to the list presented in the first paragraph of this chapter: the sales and marketing function, finance and payroll, human resources, legal and security issues, computer systems, management and administration, and something to sell.

As I am neither a lawyer nor an accountant, I will not be going into detail here but simply pointing out what you must be aware of. These are critical, and I will reference resources here and on my Web site.

In the commercial world, the first thing you need is something to sell—product or service needed in some segment of the market—and a sales and marketing program. You also need a corporate structure (sole proprietorship, limited liability company [LLC], limited liability partnership [LLP], C-corporation, S-corporation, and so on), a business plan, and a management structure. You will need legal advice, a human resources program, and accounting and payroll.

When you are thinking about entering the government market, you have to consider the impact on each of these areas:

- The product or service remains basically the same.
- Your sales and marketing program will require additional tools to understand the selling process (how the government buys) and tools to identify the opportunities.

- Your corporate structure may be subject to a number of issues, not the least of which would be fair executive compensation.

- Your business size may also play a role if you qualify for a small or small disadvantaged business category.

- Legal issues will now include knowledge of the FAR, D-FAR, flow-downs, and more.

- Human resources will be impacted if your company is a certain size. Issues then will include equal employment opportunity (EEO) compliance, drug-free workplace maintenance, Wage Act compliance, and more.

SALES AND MARKETING

In order to pursue government business, you have to know where the business is and how the government buys what you sell. You also have to determine the best venues for advertising, which may be quite different from your commercial marketing. We reviewed the SSQ tool in the previous chapter, and that is a good way to measure who is selling in your niche and which companies are more successful. The SSQ is one of many tools for sales and marketing.

Other services include the paid bid-tracking services such as Federal Sources (www.fedsources.com), Input (www.input .com), and Onvia (www.onvia.com). This is not a comprehensive list by any means, but these are each nationally recognized. I prefer Onvia because it covers federal, state, and local bids, while the others focus on federal.

On the free-service side, you can follow bid announcements at the federal level by going to www.fbo.gov, which we also discussed before.

You can use the OSDBU at each federal agency. You can visit in person, call in for advice, or attend the occasional in-agency event. Many federal small business offices host regular meetings where managers from other offices in their agency come in to explain program requirements, how the agency works, upcoming needs, and the like. You can also approach regional federal offices regardless of where you are located, and most of these will have small business advocates.

LOCAL RESOURCES

Starting local is always a good option. Local government options can start with local small business development centers, which can be found by visiting http://www.sbdcnet.org. These SBDCs are located all over the country and are supported by the SBA. Often, they are found as part of universities or local colleges or as part of a county or municipal economic development office. Regardless, these can help you identify local governmental activities. Small business development centers can be found in all 50 states, the District of Columbia, Guam, and the U.S. Virgin Islands.

Another resource available in most states is procurement technical assistance centers, or PTACs (pronounced "pee-tacks"), which are sponsored by the DoD and are designed to provide small businesses (and others) with counseling services and education on pursuing government business. In total, there are 94 PTACs, and they are located in most states, as well as Guam and Puerto Rico. You can find details at www.aptac-us.org.

The SBDCs and PTACs are helpful for learning the basics of doing business with the government and are good places to start. But do not think you have the entire picture after going through any of the courses offered.

One more way to gauge local federal activity is to pay a Web visit to one of the 28 federal executive boards (www.feb.gov). The federal executive boards are located in major metropolitan areas around the country where there is a significant amount of federal government activity. Each board has a Web site that lists the member agencies, often along with links to the local Web sites. The members are all within a limited geographic proximity. This allows you to see the breadth and depth of federal activity in your immediate area. It also helps you to gauge the potential for doing business locally and to identify those you may need to meet. Start developing relationships with people who you can actually meet locally without traveling to Washington, DC.

I tie all these together by using the paid service GovSearch, available from Carroll Publishing (www.carrollpub.com). GovSearch is an online directory of over 350,000 federal, state, and local government employees around the country; nearly 1,000 federal organization charts; the budget filings that are required by the OMB; and more. These filings (Exhibit 300, the Capitol Asset Plan, and Exhibit 53, the IT Plans) are required filings from each federal agency. They map out the future expenditures of that agency so that you can see where they want to spend their budget. There are other features to GovSearch that are helpful, including information on expenditures by product category by agency. Call Carroll Publishing and have Gordon Peil give you a free tour of the tool. I have been using it for several years, and it keeps getting better with each new feature.

All right, now the hard stuff. If you've ever seen *MythBusters* on television, they occasionally include the disclaimer, "We're professionals, and we do this for a living. Don't try this at home." That is my advice as we get into legal, accounting, and HR issues as a contractor.

FINANCE, PAYROLL, AND PERSONNEL

June Jewell is president of Acumen Advisors, an advisory firm specializing in the government market. Her LinkedIn profile includes this line: *We specialize in helping our clients implement business development and financial management systems and processes to increase project profitability and win more business.*

Among other things, Acumen Advisors helps companies install the software that aids them in managing the government side of the business. They are Deltek's leading partner (more on Deltek later). When I asked her (four hours before the beginning of a holiday weekend) for a short list of issues facing the novice contractor, here was her initial take:

> Our clients are usually trying to solve the following problems:
>
> Enforcement of time sheet policies with employees—government contractors must have their employees enter daily and follow a set procedure for making changes. The DCAA [Defense Contract Audit Agency] can come in and perform a desk audit at any time. Some clients have been caught because they are not enforcing these policies and don't have adequate policies and procedures that are well documented for employees. It is a requirement to have these policies documented, and if you do, you stand a higher chance of passing an audit.
>
> Other issues surrounding DCAA compliance include handling of unallowable expenses; proper structure and calculation of indirect rates and allocation to projects (this is also important for maximizing the revenue on contracts and also to be competitive on bids); complying with all contract FAR clauses, including warning clients when you have hit 75 percent complete on the contract value; reporting—giving auditors the reports they want in the way they want them (this includes the incurred cost submission reports); maintaining proper records; billing correctly; and managing the difference between actual and provisional (contract) indirect rates.

This was after a brief exchange of e-mails. I know her list could go on and on.

When you are a government contractor, not only do you need to know about the regulations, but you also have to learn to deal with them in the most expedient way and maintain compliance. For example, regardless of how many employees you have, you need to know the federal Fair Labor Standards Act (FLSA). Government contracts are heavily regulated, and if a contractor fails to comply with any of the pertinent contract laws or regulations, the liability can be *substantial*.

A ton of wage and hour policy contractor information and links are available at the Department of Labor Web site (www.dol.gov), including links to the public laws (USC 3701, etc.) and pertinent references to the Code of Federal Regulations (CFR; especially 29 CFR 5). Here are just a few examples of records that must be maintained (and yes, some items are included in June's list, but it is advice from the Department of Labor):

- Job descriptions
- Job postings and advertisements
- Records of job offers
- Applications and resumes
- Tests and results
- Interview notes
- Written employment policies and procedures
- Personnel files

And speaking of personnel files, you need to keep employment records for two years from the date of the making of the personnel record or the personnel action, whichever comes last.

Contractors with less than 150 employees or a contract valued lower than $150,000 only have to keep records for one year.

As a contractor, you need to file the Standard Form 100, Employer Identification Report (EEO-1 Report), by September 30 (end of FY) every year. This provides the number of employees for your company by race, ethnicity, and gender for each of nine job categories. This and more is covered in the federal FLSA.

The FLSA and the laws of each of the 50 states regulate what constitutes "overtime." This FSLA has been with us since the 1930s, but congressional intervention over the years has made it more complicated, especially in matters concerning small business.

Before we leave the world of employment, here are a few basic EEO regulations for federal contractors:

- Don't discriminate.
- Post EEO posters around the workplace.
- Include the EEO compliance tagline in all employment ads.
- Make all records available during EEO evaluations and complaint disputes.

LEGAL, ACCOUNTING, AND ETHICAL ISSUES

Federal Publications Seminars open one of their online brochures with this line: "There is accounting . . . and there is government contract accounting." It implies that this is a different world, and it is. Here are just a few of the issues you face in legal and accounting areas:

- Regulatory compliance
- Government contract audit support
- Cost proposal support
- Accounting systems implementation and support
- Cost allocation structures
- Claims and contract administration
- Cost accounting standards
- Litigation support

At this point, you may well be asking yourself if it is worth the hassle. The answer is no, probably not for everyone. The oversight in federal contracting is onerous, duplicative, and irritating, not to mention expensive. Right now, these are the very issues your competitors want you think about and act on. They want you to leave this minute and say, "Whew, we escaped that bullet!"

From the government side, you have the DCAA and inspector general looking over your shoulder or perhaps a GSA auditor looking to verify that the industrial funding fee (IFF) has been paid. From your company's side, you may have investors or other advisors and employees telling you what needs to be done.

Right now, I want to focus on the following point that I took from the Deltek Web site, one of the firms providing accounting and compliance software to the government contracting community:

> Contrary to the belief prevalent in many companies, the issue of accounting system compliance does not really revolve around the software itself. Certainly a key consideration is the functionality and capability of the software employed. Even more important, though, is the network of practices and procedures required for compliance. And most important of all are the internal control mechanisms that monitor and enforce them.

And then there are the *ethical* regulations that are defined by the U.S. Office of Government Ethics (www.usoge.gov). The one issue here that seems to cause many problems is gifts.

While there are a number of gray areas in the ethical arena, here is an example of a bad move.

Several years back, when the book *Reengineering the Corporation* came out, some people at the headquarters of Digital Equipment Corporation decided that it would be an appropriate gift for senior federal information technology managers, at the time called information resource managers, or IRMs. There were about 800 or so senior IRMs, and Digital sent each a copy of the book.

Very shortly thereafter, they received a letter from an inspector general indicating that they had violated the ethical threshold for gift-giving and that they were to collect all the books they sent out ASAP. If they did not comply, they were told that they may face losing contracts.

At that time, the legal gratuity level for gifts was $20, tax included, and the book was well over the threshold. The general guidelines for acceptable gratuities when working with a federal employee include the following:

- Gifts under $20
- Refreshments during a meeting (nothing lavish)
- Invitations to an event
- Discounts available to everyone

All of your employees who work directly with the government should be aware of these restrictions, as should any subcontractors and consultants working on your behalf.

Here is exactly what the Office of Government Ethics says on the matter of gifts from outside sources (www.usoge.gov/common_ethics_issues/gifts_outsidesources.aspx):

Executive branch employees are subject to restrictions on the gifts that they may accept from sources outside the government. Generally they may not accept gifts that are given because of their official positions or that come from certain interested sources ("prohibited sources"). Prohibited sources include persons (or an organization made up of such persons) who—

- are seeking official action by, are doing business or seeking to do business with, or are regulated by the employee's agency.
- have interests that may be substantially affected by performance or nonperformance of the employee's official duties.

In addition, an employee can never solicit or coerce the offering of a gift, or accept a gift in return for being influenced in the performance of an official act. Nor can an employee accept gifts so frequently that a reasonable person might think that the employee was using public office for private gain.

There are a number of exceptions to the ban on gifts from outside sources. These allow an employee to accept—

- a gift valued at $20 or less, provided that the total value of gifts from the same person is not more than $50 in a calendar year.
- a gift motivated solely by a family relationship or personal friendship.
- a gift based on an employee's or his spouse's outside business or employment relationships, including a gift customarily provided by a prospective employer as part of *bona fide* employment discussions.
- a gift provided in connection with certain political activities.
- gifts of free attendance at certain widely attended gatherings, provided that the agency has determined that attendance is in the interest of the agency.
- modest refreshments (such as coffee and donuts), greeting cards, plaques and other items of little intrinsic value.
- discounts available to the public or to all government employees, rewards and prizes connected to competitions open to the general public.

There are other exceptions, including exceptions for awards and honorary degrees, certain discounts and other benefits, attendance at certain social events, and meals, refreshments, and entertainment in foreign countries.

These exceptions are subject to some limitations on their use. For example, an employee can never solicit or coerce the offering of a gift. Nor can an employee use exceptions to accept gifts on such a frequent basis that a reasonable person would believe that the employee was using public office for private gain.

If an employee has received a gift that cannot be accepted, the employee may return the gift or pay its market value. If the gift is perishable (e.g. a fruit basket or flowers) and it is not practical to return it, the gift may, with approval, be given to charity or shared in the office.*

When Uncle Sam outlines the rules, it is best to stay inside the boundaries.

WHEN, WHERE, AND HOW TO GET PROFESSIONAL ASSISTANCE: FINDING AND SELECTING OUTSIDE VENDORS

There are outside vendors for all disciplines in the government market: advertising and marketing, public relations, sales, business development, bid and proposal, capture, accounting, legal issues, security clearances and SCIFs, and on and on. Keep in mind that not all outside vendors are equal. Some excel in their areas of expertise; others are simply good, some are not quite so good, and so on.

First, how do you know *when* you need help? You know you need accounting help when the GSA or other government auditing agency shows up and your books do not answer the questions they have. At this point, you may also require legal help.

---

*Source: 5 C.F.R. [Code of Federal Regulations] §§ 2635.201–205 (http://www.usoge.gov/laws_regs/regulations/5cfr2635.aspx)

The fact is that you need the infrastructure in place *before* you start. You need to find the right advisors, regardless of where you live, and start getting some feedback. Interview multiple lawyers and accounting firms. Get and check the recommendations for each. Contact your local PTAC and see if they have a list of local support services they can recommend. Many of the DC-based legal and accounting firms that specialize in the government market have regional offices.

I have seen requests for accounting, legal, and other recommendations on LinkedIn in many of the government-contracting-focused groups. Another way to find these advisors is to read the pertinent trade publications and check out those who are writing the articles—publications such as the *Public Contract Law Journal* (available at www.abanet.org/contract/operations/lawjournal/journal.html). Check out those teaching courses at local universities and the for-profit seminar companies. Do not be passive about this; you want and need the best advice available.

You can accomplish the same thing with both online and offline networking groups. The AFCEA, ACT/IAC, Northern Virginia Technology Council (NVTC), Tech Council of Maryland, ASBC, and others will have companies that service contractors as members. Some of these groups have subgroups, or special interest groups, where these consultants are more easily identified. By attending any of the meetings, you will be able find a few. The more active consultants will be more visible in these groups, often heading a special interest group.

You can certainly use social networks such as LinkedIn to find some prospective consultants. If you are in any of the government groups on LinkedIn, simply post a query in the discussion area asking what legal and accounting advice people are getting. You will usually receive recommendations from clients and some messages from lawyers and accountants. LinkedIn, the Federal Contractor Network, and GovLoop all have groups such as federal government contractors groups, Government Market Master groups, and GSA and Veterans Affairs Schedules groups, each of which will have lawyers and accountants as members. LinkedIn has literally hundreds of groups focusing on all aspects of the government market, including groups for marketing, program management, bid and proposal, GSA Schedules, and more. Many of these can provide you with the names of potential sources.

After you have your list of potential service providers, you need to determine the *criteria* for selecting the vendor you require. The major elements to consider are their track records, how familiar they are with your niche, their prices, how they work with their clients, and their availability.

The track records of the individuals or companies on your list are the first things you need to look into. How long have they been doing this, and who have they worked with? What kind of references do they have?

You can write your initial review for each reference by using LinkedIn. Using LinkedIn can also help you reference both the company and the individual. LinkedIn profiles will often indicate how long a company has been around. This service can also provide information on what other people think about any individual working for the company, as long as they are connected. LinkedIn allows people who are directly connected to recommend one another for areas of expertise. These recommendations are usually available to read.

Other aspects of the vendor profile that might prove helpful are how many (and which) groups they belong to and how many "Best Answer" ratings they have if they participate in the LinkedIn Q&A feature.

And when all else fails, there is always the option of asking your peers for their opinions. There is nothing like word of mouth from people you trust.

There is always more to the equation, but this should get you started.

Before we end this chapter, I want to share a word of caution—and a story. Noncompliance with a contract can get you in trouble. If the noncompliance is thought to be intentional, the hot water gets hotter and deeper. Sometimes, though, the government offers you a settlement, some sort of fine, which you pay; then you promise that things will be better, and life goes on.

In October 2003, GovConnection, a subsidiary of PC Connection, had their GSA Schedule contract suspended for 30 days. GovConnection met with the GSA several times to resolve whatever the issue was. Rumors were flying, and competitors were ecstatic. By November, there was no resolution, and the suspension was not lifted. Apparently, noncompliant products supposedly had been shipped in place of products that were requested. Regardless of the validity of the claim, the upshot was that GovConnection lost a GSA Schedule valued at about $32 million per year.

This issue could have been solved simply by paying the fine.

Although GovConnection did get a new GSA Schedule, it took over a year to receive. At that point, they had to rebuild their GSA sales funnel and find replacements for some of those who left. GovConnection continued to do business with the government without a Schedule, as they had other contracts, but it hurt them nonetheless.

This is not an isolated issue. The GSA has gone after several contractors for both valid and silly reasons. It seems as though GSA lawyers operate in an intellectual vacuum when it comes to understanding how business occurs. The issue of offering incentives to more productive business partners has been viewed, on occasion, as something akin to kickbacks.

I faced a ridiculous situation with a former client recently, where the GSA went back more than a decade to claim that rebates were owed, when clearly, they were not. We can only hope that their education becomes more complete as they interact with the contracting community.

YOUR TO-DO LIST

1. Start your search early for advisors in legal, accounting, and personnel areas.
2. Develop as much of the infrastructure as possible if you have decided the government market is for you.
3. Make certain your regular advisors in these areas are brought up to speed on contracting issues.
4. If for any reason you find yourself in hot water and are offered a fine in lieu of a suspension, seriously consider paying the fine.
5. If you need recommendations for any professionals in this market, give me a call or send me an e-mail.
6. Some recommendations will be posted at www.Government MarketMaster.com.

CHAPTER 5

Aligning Marketing, Sales, and Business Development

Regardless of the validity, government people feel their needs are different from the commercial market, and they like to be treated accordingly. Understand the culture—the "service to the citizen" purpose as opposed to a profit motive. These and other nuances are keys to the success of your marketing, sales, and business development (BD) efforts.

Marketing, sales, and business development in the government market are different, and the executives at your company must understand this. The marketing formulas that work elsewhere will probably not have the desired results here.

Briefly, here are the roles. A *business development professional* is a person whose mission is to find contracts to participate in as a prime or subcontractor. They are habitual networkers and information seekers. The better ones are insatiable information absorbers. They possess both technical knowledge and an understanding of the best fit for your company on any given deal, including an awareness of that which is not a fit.

Salespeople are, well, salespeople. But in the government market, they not only must possess the knowledge and skills to sell from the contracts you currently have, but they also need to understand when the customer is offering them an opening to develop a new contract—perhaps a BPA off your GSA or a task order off another vehicle. They understand the needs of the customer, their buying habits, and the sales cycle.

Marketing professionals in the government market are those who try to understand and balance corporate needs, the requirements of the sales force, and the long-range goals of the BD staff. They assimilate this and try to provide the best marketing venues and programs to support each effort, keeping in mind the overall corporate goals.

It is also critical for all marketing efforts to stay well within the ethical bounds set by the government. As we have seen, when the corporate level intervenes, this can go awry. According to a story that I have heard from more than one source, the manufacturer of a secure communications device worked long and hard to get their product on a contract that got the device on Air Force One. Without understanding the repercussions, someone at headquarters (HQ) issued a press release touting this milestone. Within a week, the device had been removed from Air Force One. Some wins we keep to ourselves. Though I was never able to verify the story, it is certainly believable.

Here is another typical scenario I get from the front lines. I receive a call from the federal sales manager here in the DC area. His or her company is not based in the Washington, DC, area, and the government is only one market the company targets. He or she tells me that his or her boss, the vice president of sales at HQ, has tasked him or her with a lead generation program, but he or she has been given the marketing template from which to operate—the same template that is to be used by all market segments: a direct-mail package that had generated leads at the chief information officer (CIO) level in their B2B midtier financial market. Because of the success of the package in the financial market, the company is rolling it out to all other market segments, including Fed and SLED. The metrics showed an above-average conversion rate on the leads generated. The main job of the federal sales manager is to select the "right list" targeting government CIOs.

The mail package is comprised of a slick brochure, a case study, some testimonials, and a link to a landing page at the company Web site. The mailer is 9-by-12 inches and is a little bulky due to the brochure. As necessary, keywords in the text of the package can be changed to "government-ize" the mailing.

Here's where a little knowledge is truly a dangerous thing. The vice president at HQ has enough knowledge to recognize that the sales language needs to be adapted to the market but not enough knowledge to grasp that oversized mailers targeting federal HQ activities in and around Washington, DC (where most of the federal CIOs are located), are sent out to be irradiated prior to being delivered to the intended office. The anthrax scare several years back put in place a policy that requires incoming mail at federal HQ activities be sent out for irradiation. Regardless of the success of this mail package in other markets, it was doomed from the outset not to be a lead generator for government. Once a brochure is irradiated, it looks like papier-mâché.

In another instance, I frequently hear about corporate sales directors tasking government sales personnel with generating end-of-quarter sales without understanding the federal buying cycle. This is not uncommon, especially for publicly traded companies.

While these examples may not fit how your company operates, if your company is not based in the Washington, DC area, and if it is not solely focused on the government market, educating the corporate office becomes a significant part of the task.

Assumptions from HQ regarding the viability and ease of entry into the government market are rampant. These are often driven by factors that have absolutely nothing to do with the realities of the government market but have urgency nonetheless, generated by the following:

- Headquarters needs sales by the end of the quarter (this happens every quarter).
- A board member heard one of the "good" myths about the federal market from someone sitting next to him or her on an airplane (this one has occurred several times).

- An article in a business magazine discusses the "great" small business set-aside program in a 600-word article (an article way too short to explain anything).
- Someone at HQ has heard of the "end-of-federal-FY spending spree" and wants in.
- At a Vistage meeting, a CEO from a totally unrelated industry indicated some easy success in selling to the government.

Ideas generated from multiple semireliable and unreliable sources spawn irrational exuberance over the possibility of winning government business. Unrealistic time frames and impatience can kill a potentially good government program. So, where do you go for reliable information on marketing, sales, and business development?

There are basically two types of companies selling to the government: product companies and service companies. Sometimes, these overlap—a product vendor with a service component or a service company that has a product component. While the marketing for each may have similarities, there will be significant differences in the marketing mix and in the audiences targeted.

In this chapter, we will deal mostly with traditional marketing methods. In Chapter 11, I will discuss the Web 2.0 marketing elements.

MARKETING, SALES, AND BUSINESS DEVELOPMENT FOR PROFESSIONAL SERVICES

The government acquires services almost exclusively through contracts, including the GSA Schedule. There are hundreds of companies vying in each service category for this business. And once again, many companies sell only to the government and are quite experienced in pursuing this business with a significant measure of success. These are the companies whose task orders will never show up at www.fbo.gov. These are also the companies whose ability in the bid and proposal process, regardless of how tightly their skill matches the requirement, far exceeds the skills of the novice or near-novice. Not only do they have an in-house team, but they will also bring in the heavyweight outside resources to win the larger contracts.

On the GSA Schedule, the main Schedule for services is MOBIS (Schedule 874). Here (from the GSA Web site) you will find survey services; acquisition management support (yes, the government gets help in procurement and lots of it); consulting services; facilitation services (facilitation and related decision support services to agencies); training services (off-the-shelf or customized off-the-shelf training packages to meet specific agency needs related to management, organizational and business improvement services, certification programs, and even degree programs); support products used in support of services offered (including workbooks, manuals, slides, videos, software programs, etc.); privatization support services and documentation (support, assistance, and documentation generation required in the conduct of OMB Circular A-76); and program integration and program management services (services to manage and integrate various management and business improvement programs and projects that may or may not be the result of MOBIS recommendations). These services may include projects internal to federal agencies; project management that connects and maintains the liaison between multiple contractors; the monitoring of multiple projects; expert services supporting agency alternative dispute resolution (ADR) programs, both formal and informal—and it goes on and on.

In FY 2009, the MOBIS Schedule accounted for $4,376,556,818, and there were 2,096 contractors. As usual, the top 100 contract holders took over 60 percent of the dollars awarded.

In order to become a provider of professional services to the government (federal, state, or local), there are several things you must consider.

First, as the C-level, you must understand that most professional services sales are long-cycle sales. If they are long in the commercial world, the likelihood is that they will be longer in the government market. Pursuing this business often requires experienced BD professionals as opposed to sales personnel.

Good BD professionals start by matching your core strengths with agency requirements. Then, they identify current contracts or emerging opportunities where the agency buys (or may buy) this type of service.

Third, the BD people meet regularly with the government officials and contractors likely to bid (or the contractor currently holding the contract). If they don't already have a relationship for this opportunity, they start developing multiple relationships and communicating your company strengths. They set up meetings with both the clients and the contractor to introduce your various team members, further developing the relationship and more deeply establishing your area of expertise. The more your staff knows about the client or prospective client, the higher the comfort level for the buyer.

It would also be the role of the BD professional to go out and find opportunities for you to bid as the prime contractor—if you are ready for prime time. If not, subcontracting is not only a viable option, but it is another way for the agency to get to know you.

One caveat on business development: BD professionals are not driven by end-of-FY spending like salespeople. They are more interested in becoming part of the program once awarded, and then letting the sales force take over and maximize the value of the contract.

All of the collateral material used by your BD staff has to be geared to the public sector. What you did for a for-profit company or a nonprofit association may have a bearing on the needs of the client, but unless your material directly addresses their needs and requirements as a government agency, the likelihood of you winning business is radically reduced.

Bob Lohfeld, CEO of the Lohfeld Consulting Group, put it this way: "You need a well-thought-out strategy to differentiate your offering from others and a well-defined value proposition that addresses the government's needs. Commercial selling jargon like 'increase your profits' will fall on deaf ears with the government buyer, whereas 'improve service to the citizen' may be just what the government wants to hear." Your collateral material has to address the public sector directly.

It is often easier to start off as a subcontractor to a larger firm after establishing your area of expertise with both the government customer and the contractor. While the terms and conditions (including the hourly pay) may not be great, this will help you establish your past performance record in the public sector. If the government customer likes your work, it becomes much easier to find more work.

This is not a quick turnaround arena. Be prepared to devote time and resources if you are serious about pursuing professional services business in the government market.

The government market also suffers from a cyclical review and reevaluation of what the government needs and how it should get it. The current debate centers on outsourcing, which is the use of government contractors for "inherently governmental" work. As this debate goes on, the use of contractors in these roles grows. The reality is that there are just not enough personnel in the government to do all the things government agencies are supposed to do and to get them done well. The services side of selling to the government is huge and will likely stay that way, regardless of the debates centered on outsourcing and what is or is not inherently governmental.

From my perspective, the debates give politicians and presidential appointees something to argue about and perhaps allow them to appear as though they are doing something useful.

Back to the point at hand, the key steps in the process of selling services to the government are as follows:

1. Match your area of expertise with an agency's needs.
2. Identify the contract or contracts that are designed to fill those needs.

3. Have the right personnel in place—people who already have skills and relationships.

4. Support the sales personnel with the right collateral material.

5. Understand the long-term nature of the sale.

6. Set your BD professional loose in the market to match your core strengths with current and emerging opportunities in the agencies where you are a fit.

7. Identify each of the opportunities you can most likely win (as prime or sub or via the GSA Schedule).

8. Meet with the key government and industry people involved in those opportunities and set up meetings with your key personnel.

9. Develop the necessary relationships and further establish your area of expertise.

10. Pursue and capture the business.

11. Perform these steps over and over again (rinse and repeat).

While this is somewhat oversimplified, it is the basic process. The marketing that supports the sales and business development has to be in place before and during the process.

But none of this guarantees business will occur. In my interview with BD master Bob Davis, he tells a story of briefing senior management on an opportunity for which his company was a very tight technical match. After going through his carefully prepared PowerPoint presentation, someone at the briefing asked a direct question: "Are we going to win this business?"

Bob replied no, and when asked to explain, he said, "The customer does not know us, and they want someone they have worked with before." Go back to step number three: When you are pursuing contracts or selling services via your GSA Schedule, it really helps to have people in place who have relationships with the agency awarding the business.

Where does the marketing fit in the BD process? First and foremost, it plays a role in researching to match your services with agency needs. For upcoming agency needs, each agency has to file an OMB 300. Section 300 of the OMB Circular A-11 establishes policy for planning, budgeting, and acquiring and managing federal capital assets and provides guidance for budget justification and reporting requirements for major IT investments and major non-IT capital assets. In plain language, this is the 12- to 24-month outlook for agency spending. You need to know where the money is likely to be allocated, and for what, in order to make informed decisions about where your marketing dollars really need to be spent. Too many marketing efforts are broad in nature—created by ad agencies or novices with little, if any, government experience—and they either miss the target audience or broadside many market segments.

As marketing consultant Fred Diamond likes to remind me, marketing dollars not tied to sales results are wasted.

So, once the determination is made of what agencies to target and why, specific targeted marketing programs can be formulated to support sales and business development. The elements for these programs could include the following:

- In-agency tabletop expos, which are usually half-day exhibiting opportunities.

- Targeted public relations outreach, designed to get your key staff into the publications pertinent to your market niche and into specific articles that highlight your area of expertise.

- Pages at your Web site for each contract. The Web site is especially important, because it is a primary source of information for any of your customers. Do not have a one-size-fits-all Web site that is for both your commercial and B2G efforts, regardless of how similar the needs of each might be.

- White papers, both executive and technical. You can host these on your own Web site or have them linked at trade publication sites.

- Technology-specific events that focus on a niche technology (cloud computing, information assurance, the Information Technology Infrastructure Library [ITIL], or some other specific area) and that attract those in government from many agencies who share the same technical concerns.
- Networking events you can sponsor.
- Agency-sponsored events that appeal to your audience.
- Focused sponsorships (ads) in e-newsletters targeting your niche. Most trade publications have e-news programs with sponsorships available. You can also start your own e-newsletter.
- Targeted banner ads on the trade publication Web sites. If you can buy the ads that show up in pertinent search results, this is even better.
- Marketing dollars allocated to joining and participating in industry groups such as the AFCEA, the IAC, TechAmerica, the Professional Services Council, the ASBC, and others. It's a long list (see Appendix 2).
- Downloads (pdf files) developed for your services. Have both a one-page overview and a longer version available on your Web site. Your one-pagers should include your main areas of expertise, NAICS code(s), PSC, SIN, all contracts the services are available on, key personnel on the contract, and contact information. All pertinent collateral should be made available on your Web site as well.
- Knowledge of when and if the end of FY will play a role in a particular sale and support for activity that will help close the sale.

On the services side, keep in mind that the main role of marketing is to help sales and BD people identify and nurture relationships with key influencers and to create awareness about your company's role in that niche. These influencers may include the government, the industry (prime contractors you want to work with), the press, and others.

It is very helpful if marketing staffers sit in on sales and BD meetings. The more your marketing staff understands both the sales and BD processes and the agency's targets of opportunity, the more likely your marketing investment will pay dividends.

SALES AND MARKETING FOR PRODUCTS

Let's assume you have mapped out what products you are going to sell and how you are going sell to the government. For product vendors under the micropurchase threshold, this can be open market (no contracts). For others, it can be the GSA Schedule or another GWAC, such as the National Institutes of Health Electronic Commodity Store (NIH ECS 3) contract or the NASA SEWP contract. How do you market to the largest buyer in the world? Where do you start?

The first thing to do is to make certain that your company Web site is government friendly. A specific click-through section of your site clearly labeled "government" is a good starting place. Web sites are always among the first places a government buyer looks for information. If your Web site is not sufficiently government friendly, the buyer will move on.

Inside the government portion of your site, you begin by clearly stating your value proposition(s) in ways that address the public sector. Remember, some of what motivates them is different than what motivates a typical business client. Recognize the differences from their perspective. There is no profit motive in the public sector; its purpose is mission fulfillment or service to the citizen. Other factors, especially for selling products, may be the same: How fast can you deliver it? What is your customer service policy? Your return policy?

If you sell on the open market (no contracts), you will be targeting the SmartPay (government credit card) business and focusing on orders under $3,000. B2B catalog companies and others in the transactional business can do well in the micropurchase arena. Downloading the SmartPay logo from the GSA Web site to include under your government section is always a good idea and a good starting place. Go to www.gsa.gov/smartpay to find the SmartPay logo.

As a product vendor, it is good to emphasize that you are competitively priced, that the quality of the product is good, and that you can deliver quickly. If you have great customer service, say so. While it is difficult to differentiate commodity products, it is not difficult to differentiate the company selling the products.

One company that does this well is Lab Safety (www.lss.com), which is a vendor of lab and industrial safety products. On their Web site, scroll to the bottom of the home page to find the "LSS.com Resource Centers" and click on "Government." The government page at Lab Safety starts with the phrase *SmartPay proudly welcomed here* and the credit card logo. This is followed by other differentiators that Lab Safety delivers on: real people answer the phone, product selection is outstanding, prices are guaranteed for a year, fast shipping is offered inside the continental United States, and the store (Web site) is open 24 hours a day, 7 days a week, 365 days a year.

After that, Lab Safety offers a link to their catalog, introduces both the tech support and technical experts, and then provides Web links and "EZFacts," which are really cool. With these, Lab Safety has cross-referenced the CFR with selected product areas to help the government procurement officer justify purchasing specific items. These product areas happen to be the areas in which Lab Safety offers a product that fits the regulation. In effect, they are providing purchasers with documented justification for purchasing that product. This is brilliant.

Lab Safety sells exclusively on the open market. I do not know what their government sales are, but what they have done with the government section of their Web site is excellent and should be emulated by those selling on the open market.

If you have opted to obtain a GSA Schedule contract, a good site to emulate is that of ATD-American (www.atdamerican.com), an established vendor of office furniture to commercial, institutional, and government accounts.

The ATD home page offers an array of popular office furniture, some clearly labeled "Best Sellers." On the left side of the home page is the newsletter sign-up option (prominent at the top left), then the "Search" box, the product categories, and help and information on the company. In the right-side column is a featured product, a list of the top five best sellers, a "Contact Us Now" box, and places to request or order from the catalog.

When you click on "Customer Service" under the "Help and Info" heading in the left-hand column, you are forwarded to a page that offers a variety of links from which to choose, including "5 Reasons to Buy from ATD," an offer for free design services and swatches, information about their GSA contracts and rating, details on nationwide installation services, and more.

When you click through to the GSA contracts and rating pages, ATD announces their "exceptional" vendor rating awarded by the GSA and lists the major furniture suppliers they carry, along with the contract numbers for easy ordering.

Both Lab Safety and ATD treat government buyers as a separate market. This indicates to potential buyers that they are dealing with an experienced government vendor. Both vendors use key industry phrases for the products throughout their Web sites—the same terms people would be searching for. They both also reference SmartPay, which may be used by government buyers as a search term. Without a strong home page for government product buyers, your product marketing efforts will go nowhere.

Here's a short checklist for marketing products to the government:

- Have pdf downloads for each product available from your Web site. If applicable, include the contract(s) the product is available on.
- Start your own government e-news program. Include an "opt-in" box on the home page of your government site.

- Make certain your sales staff is adequately prepared to sell to the public sector.

- Government-ize your Web site and collateral material.

- Participate in the conferences, in-agency tabletops, and other venues where your prospects will be in attendance.

- Support your outbound sales staff by providing current directories. I use and recommend Carroll Publishing's GovSearch.

- Advertise year-round, but heavy up as you approach the end of the FY (federal FY is October 1 through September 30).

- Your in-bound sales staff should be on duty through midnight in the last time zone on the day of September 30. The U.S. government has personnel all over the world, and they will be placing orders that need to be processed by midnight in their time zones.

HOW TO MARKET YOUR SMALL CONTRACTING BUSINESS: NETWORKING

It is impossible to overstate the value of developing and maintaining key relationships in the government market. The first line in my book *Government Marketing Best Practices* is, "This market, any market, is about relationships." For really small businesses and others with extremely limited budgets, the best form of marketing is face-to-face networking.

Washington, DC, networking maven Ardell Fleeson and I have discussed the topic of traditional (face-to-face) networking several times on my radio show, and I have gleaned these thoughts from those shows and our many conversations. We even cut a CD on the topic, which I listen to regularly. I often include it as a bonus when I sell other CD programs. We all need good tips on networking, and in DC, Ardell is among the best.

Face-to-face networking is a major factor for success in the government market, and every day in the DC area, there are hundreds of places where formal and informal networking occurs. One of the hot spots for networking is the Tower Club in Vienna, Virginia. You can argue that starting at 7 AM every day, networking does not stop until the last patron leaves the dining room after dinner. When I walk through the main dining room, I can see people making introductions and closing deals.

This issue is critical for small businesses. A small company has fewer feet on the street, and selecting the right venues on where to meet key people becomes critical to survival and growth. You have to make time to get out and meet people in the government market—preferably those who can help you grow your business. This has to become a regular part of your business week. Yes, it takes time; everything about running a business takes time.

So, how do you select the proper venues for your business? Here are some tips to help you get started:

1. Where do you currently spend your time looking for partners, customers, and so forth? The first thing to do is to determine *who* you are looking for; then you can start figuring out *where* to find them. If you know some of them, simply ask.

2. There are major networking groups in our market: the AFCEA (national and local chapters), TechAmerica (formerly the Information Technology Association of America [ITAA]), the Professional Services Council, and ACT/IAC. There are also smaller, but not necessarily less influential, groups: the Northern Virginia Tech Council, Women in Technology, the Tech Council of Maryland, the ASBC, the Potomac Officers Club, Government Market Master (my new networking forum), and many others. While you cannot spend time at all of these, if you have answered question number one properly, you might find the right group(s) on this list to add to your networking.

3. If your company is driven by a technology niche (information security, information assurance, etc.), you need to find the venues that serve that community. Often, these are government-sponsored groups, such as the Federal Information Systems Security Educators Association (FISSEA), which has representatives from all federal agencies and is hosted at the National Institutes of Standards and Technology (NIST) in Gaithersburg, Maryland.

4. Ask your best customers and business partners where they spend their networking time.

5. Ask recognized industry experts where they spend their time.

So, now you probably have at least a few networking venues queued up. Aside from making certain you have plenty of business cards, what do you need to do to prepare?

For each venue you attend, decide what you wish to accomplish: meet some new contacts, meet some specific contacts, introduce some of your contacts to some new people, start establishing some overall visibility, and so forth. Decide that you need to meet at least two or three great new contacts for each event you attend.

Now, try to get to the venue early. This way, you may be able to look at the name tags of those attending to see precisely who you'd like to meet. This can shorten the cycle of meeting those two or three new people.

Next, you need to be able to clearly, precisely, and *briefly* say what your company does. "Clearly" means using few adjectives; "precisely" means focusing on your core strength. Say something like, "We focus on information assurance," *not* a general statement like, "We are an IT services firm" or "We are a systems integrator." Finally, "briefly" means 15 to 20 seconds, max. If you go beyond that, you are assuming that the person with whom you are speaking has an interest.

Always listen to what others say to you. Remember, networking is a two-way street, so always try to help each person you meet if you expect him or her to help you. The more you help others, the more return you will get on each new relationship.

If you have met truly useful people, try to get on their calendar quickly, before the memory of meeting you fades. Breakfast or coffee is easier than lunch. The first meeting is your opportunity to bring along some information on your company, and expect them to bring some on their company or agency as well. Remember, this is a fifty-fifty situation. Do not expect to dominate the time allotted for the meeting. It is not a "selling" meeting, it is a "getting to know you" meeting.

This is a tip-of-the-iceberg overview on getting started with networking. There are several calendars of events available through various media, including the Washington Technology Web site, www.WashingtonTechnology.com. Find the calendars that best suit your niche, and ask your peers what they attend.

If you are not in Washington, DC, find the professional associations that have government contractor members and those that have government members. If you have anything to do with facilities, groups such as the International Facility Managers Association (IFMA) and the Building Owners and Managers Association (BOMA) are good venues, with chapters all over the country.

Participating in the right events remains an important component in any marketing program. However, being able to stand out at an event is not always easy. A few years back, Evan Weisel of Welz & Weisel Communications (www.w2comm .com) helped a client with a limited budget stand out at a major conference.

GOING "ALL IN" TO GENERATE KEY RELATIONSHIPS

In today's world, much interaction is done from behind a computer, and this includes using social media, but trade shows still remain very important activities at which to meet face to face with target audiences—be it the media, analysts, partners, or customers. The challenge at trade shows is that gaining people's attention is often difficult, and this is no different at the annual RSA security conference (the largest IT security event in the world). In 2007, Welz & Weisel Communications represented three security clients participating at the event that were looking to build new relationships as well as to further existing ones.

Rather than a typical cocktail hour or reception, Welz & Weisel Communications came up with the idea of hosting a poker tournament on the first night of the event. With poker growing in popularity, the thought was that this could be an excellent forum to bring people together to interact with one another over a common interest. All three clients agreed that this was definitely worth trying. Each company invited their own partners, prospects, and customers, while Welz & Weisel Communications was responsible for inviting the press and analysts to attend. They also developed cards and poker chips that had the sponsoring companies' logos on them.

About 50 attendees showed up, with 30 of them playing in the poker tournament. Of the 30 playing, about half were industry press and analysts. The tournament was free to play in, and prizes were given out to the top five finishers, with the winner awarded a 32-inch plasma television. In addition to the tournament, there was an open bar and plenty of free food.

The three companies had people dealing or playing at the different poker tables, and participants were strategically placed so that the sponsoring companies could build relationships. One benefit of playing poker is that you really get to know the other people at the table. In the end, all of the sponsoring companies and participants agreed that this was one of the best trade show events they had attended—so good that this event remains today, three years later, although the sponsoring companies have changed through the years (acquisitions are quite frequent in the security world!).

What was the return on investment? The companies' salespeople were able to meet with a number of choice prospects in an informal way while working to maintain existing relationships with customers and partners and to build relationships with the press and analysts. In fact, this event helped the sponsoring companies to stand out to the press and analysts at a very noisy event, and when following up postevent, it was a means for starting a dialog and setting up company briefings.

The cost to host this event was approximately $15,000 and was split three ways.

YOUR TO-DO LIST

1. Train your sales force on selling from government contracts. The best venues for this will be posted on the "Events" page at www.GovernmentMarketMaster.com.
2. If you need BD personnel, check them out carefully before hiring. Many of those with BD job titles once worked as salespeople.
3. Monitor your most successful competitors and emulate their programs. Sign up for a Gmail or Yahoo! e-mail account and register to receive anything issued by these competitors' Web sites: white papers, e-news—anything.
4. Support your sales, marketing, and BD staff with the tools they need: contract tracking services, online directories such as GovSearch, and memberships in various organizations.
5. Start networking with your peers in the government market.

CHAPTER 6

The Power of Relationships

Rubber meets the road in three ways: spinning tires, hitting potholes and/or creating road kill, and actually gaining traction and getting from point A to point B. The ability to develop the right relationships and to find multiple ways to maintain those relationships is how you create traction with direction.

This is a relationship-driven market—make no mistake about it. Several stories come to mind immediately when I think about the power of relationships in the government market. There is the relationship between a sales rep and a customer and between a manufacturer and the right—or wrong—reseller. There is the relationship between a prime contractor and a subcontractor or teaming partner. There are the individual relationships between people in the market, CEO to CEO, BD to BD, consultant to consultant, and on and on. There is a reputation for the company and for the individuals in the market. Each must be monitored and managed.

Early in my career in the government market, I was fortunate to meet Lynn Bateman, a no-nonsense expert in all facets of contracting with the government. From the mid-1970s through the early 1990s, she was one of the go-to people in the market for all things pertaining to contracts.

Lynn became my default mentor. She taught me many things, but by example, she gave me my biggest lesson: Honesty, integrity, and the ability to deliver what you say you can do are the biggest things you'll have going for you. Be known for quality, and strive to be among the best. These things attract people, and that's how you start building relationships. But you have to be proactive, not passive. Simply being good at what you do is not enough. Lynn wrote for *Government Computer News*, hosted her own events, spoke at other events, and occasionally attended the other industry networking functions. Visibility is a major key.

Those lessons have served me well over the years. My personal reputation and my company's reputation have been nurtured over the years and have helped me gain a reputation in the market that is very solid. Among other things, it led to me being quoted regularly in trade publications in and outside of the government market, to speaking at industry events around the country, to serving on the board of advisors for major industry trade shows, to hosting a radio show in Washington, DC, and even to landing a book deal with John Wiley & Sons, Inc.

Like Lynn, I produce my own events, speak at other events, and attend some industry networking functions. My first book, *Government Marketing Best Practices* (2005), although self-published, did quite well, selling 9,000 copies. More important, it further established my reputation. I was the guy who literally wrote the book on government marketing.

But the reputation is only as good as my last contribution. The giving never stops. Having been in this market since the early 1980s, I have seen more than a few things that drive home the meaning of "relationship-driven market."

CUSTOMER RELATIONSHIPS

Case in point: I had a client in the mid-1990s that provided train-ing to the government. With the assistance of Patti Reardon of Government Sales Consultants, the client got a GSA Schedule, one of the earliest awarded for training by the GSA. After fine-tuning the marketing for this company to attract government customers, we ramped them up to $20 million on GSA within a couple years, which we all thought was pretty good. Things seemed to be in place, so I moved on. A few years later, I got a call from the CEO, who asked me to come back in and review the program.

The company was stuck at $20 million, and I knew the market potential was much higher. So, I poked around, inter-viewed several people internally, and looked at the marketing program. The major impediment I found was that the sales reps, all of whom were inbound telephone reps, were not assigned specific government accounts. They simply took calls in the order they came in. No salesperson was assigned to any given federal agency, regardless of the volume of busi-ness coming from each agency. While this company initially had traction, they were now in a tire-spinning mode. Without account reps assigned to each client agency, they were stuck at $20 million.

While $20 million may seem like a good amount of busi-ness, I estimated that they were losing at least that much by not having relationships in place with the major customers. My advice to that company was to assign representatives to specific agencies so that they could develop relationships with key agency personnel. They could then develop a comfort level with the agency buyers that would allow the rapport to build to a point where a real relationship could begin. Without this relationship, the ability of the company to understand the deeper training needs of the agency would never happen. You share that kind of information with people you know and trust, not with an order taker that you may never speak with again.

With this company, every time a buyer or influencer called in, they were speaking with someone different.

In order to maximize the value of any contract, you need relationships in place with the people who buy off the contract. Without these relationships, your organization is nothing more than a place that someone can call to place orders. When those relationships *are* in place, over time, the rapport that builds up allows the salesperson to better understand the current and emerging needs of the buyer and his or her office and agency. From this, more accurate sales forecasts can occur. Without the relationship, you'll never understand the breadth and depth of opportunities that agency or office might have.

The relationship between the buyer and your representative is the primary path that can lead to more revenue from that buyer and agency. Without the relationship, you might as well predicate sales by reading tea leaves. When your salespeople develop relationships, they can get the inside information they need to take a beachhead in an agency to massive growth in that account. This includes anyone on your staff who can develop relationships with anyone on the client side.

That information can come in the form of a customer mentioning that a new agency contract is being considered, that the agency is going to be purchasing more from the GSA Schedule, or that a BPA might be a nice thing to have. A BPA is a variation of your GSA offering, developed for a specific client for products the client feels they may require in some quantity over a fixed time period. Although it is an IDIQ (no money assigned), it does provide a better chance for you to get more business from a specific agency.

CHANNEL RELATIONSHIPS

The same thing is true for a company that develops relationships with manufacturers. Many companies use channel partners to sell to the government. The reasons vary, but resellers often have everything in place that a manufacturer would need, including contracts, staff, relationships, and experience. The resellers range in size from companies like multibillion dollar CDW (and CDW-G) to small mom-and-pop shops with under 10 employees. The relationships each type of company is capable of building and maintaining are different.

The larger resellers will often have direct relationships with the manufacturers. They will probably use Ingram Micro or TechData as a distributor, but they will have account reps who deal directly with the major manufacturers, perhaps developing joint marketing programs and other mutually beneficial activities. On the other hand, smaller companies may develop a relationship with an account rep at one of the distributors. This does not mean the smaller firms are totally disadvantaged, but they have to approach it from a different angle.

It becomes important for small resellers to look for other ways to grow their business. One way this can happen is by leveraging their small business status when a contract calls for a small business to take the lead.

For example, CDW-G has a program they use to partner with smaller resellers. They do this when they need to partner to pursue specific opportunities. These partners fill several of the small disadvantaged business categories and are carefully screened by CDW-G before they become part of the program. The screening allows CDW-G to avoid any performance problems with the program partners.

Many larger resellers have relationships with a network of small businesses. Often, these relationships develop when a small business finds an opportunity that they are too small to go after on their own. When this happens, they need to find a larger company to partner with, and having a relationship in place expedites the process. The opportunities do not wait.

There are many different types of relationships in the government market. Here are a few key relationships, along with some illustrative stories.

C-LEVEL TO EMPLOYEES

Stability in your company is not something that escapes the market. Developing a culture that retains and rewards performance will help you grow in this or any market. It creates comfort for those who do business with you at any level. Your ability to have real relationships and conversations with your front-line employees will also keep you better aware of any pending changes at the ground level.

In the mid-1990s, I was a member of the Industry Advisory Council, and I was asked by IAC chairman Izzy Feldman to work with the National Academy of Public Administration (NAPA) in organizing its first IT conference. Izzy knew my work, as I had actually worked for him when he owned *Government Computer News*.

Through my volunteer work with NAPA, I met a number of great people. Among those I worked with on this project were Bob Greeves, who was the lead for NAPA on this project, and Olga Grkavac, industry icon and the vice president of the Information Technology Association of America (now TechAmerica). These two are still good friends and valuable connections.

After a successful conference, I was rewarded at an IAC luncheon by having a seat at the front lunch table, facing the audience from a slightly raised platform. This was recognized as a place of honor at IAC luncheons. Seated next to me was Dan Young, then-president of Federal Data Corporation (FDC). Dan is another industry icon, having mentored several CEOs when they were budding executives at FDC. We talked over lunch, and Dan asked me to come by FDC and have lunch with him.

When I met him at his office a few weeks later, I could feel a difference when I walked in the building. The receptionist was warm, and they were expecting me. When I got to Dan's office, he greeted me like an old friend. I started asking about several aspects of FDC. Everyone in the government IT market knew FDC, and I was curious. I was looking for the differentiators—those things that drove the success of FDC.

I found out that one of these factors was employee retention. I asked Dan what made FDC different, and he told me that from top to bottom, from the executive vice president to the receptionist, his retention rate was over 11 years. That was what I felt when I walked into his building in Bethesda, Maryland. Some of Dan's graduates went on to start their own companies, with some becoming industry leaders. In semi-retirement, Dan remains one of the most gracious people I've ever met.

One reason FDC was a major player was the employee retention. In the higher-end IT arena in which FDC operated, it was known by government and industry associates as a reliable partner. Having the same staff in place played a significant role in their ability to attract partners and win contracts. This was something he was clearly, and rightfully, proud of.

COMPANY REPRESENTATIVE TO GOVERNMENT

The relationship between company representatives and the government is the first type I mentioned in this chapter. It can be with a buyer, influencer, or executive in the customer organization. It is the relationship built, over time, between someone selling and someone buying. If I go to a specific store on a regular basis, I prefer dealing with someone who knows who I am. There are contractors who have sales and BD professionals who focus on single agencies and who know those agencies inside out. Because of this, the buyers and influencers in those agencies know and trust these people. They know the mission, they understand the agency culture, they are aware of the budgeting issues, and they recognize that buyers and influencers need to add value with each call they make. They speak the same language, and there is no learning curve.

When I was working with CDW-G on one visit to Chicago, I was allowed to watch and listen as a seasoned inside sales rep made his daily calls. I listened for about an hour, during which time he made contact with about seven or eight people. It was clear from the tone of each call that he had real relationships with each of those he called. Using the tried-and-true method derived from Harvey Mackay (author of *Swim with the Sharks*) and others, and using custom contact-management software developed by CDW, the rep connected on both a personal and professional level on each call, making notes on each account as he went along. Each touch deepened that relationship.

At that time, CDW had a companywide policy that involved several weeks of training on sales, products, and more before a new hire could start making his or her customer calls. Even seasoned salespeople new to the company had to complete the CDW training. Part of this training involved learning when to pass callers off to technical or product experts, people who always seemed available on short notice when they were needed.

This attention to detail was one facet of CDW-G's emergence into the top tier of government contractors. Their advertising prowess to create name recognition helped open the door, but the relationships built by the sales professionals created the revenue. The federal marketing team of Ann-Marie Clark and Lisa DeLuca directly played a major role supporting sales.

MANUFACTURER TO CHANNEL PARTNER

For a variety of reasons, it is easier and more profitable for most manufacturers to use the channel when selling to the government. The channel is comprised of resellers, manufacturers' reps, and to a lesser degree, systems integrators. There are many resellers in the government market, ranging from those that sell thousands of different products—such as CDW-G, PC Mall, GovConnection, GTSI, and others—down to much smaller resellers that also sell hundreds or thousands of products.

Somewhere in this mix, we find what I call the "boutique reseller," a reseller that sells a limited number of products, usually those that address a specific need in the market: online publishing, distance learning, security, storage, financial management, open source, cloud computing, and on and on. The areas in which the boutique companies work are either already hot or close to being hot.

As specialists in hot niches, some of these boutique resellers gain massive traction—if they have the right relationships.

Craig Abod started Carahsoft Technology Corporation in 2004. His personal pedigree included building the Silicon Graphics (SGI) business for Falcon Microsystems under the tutelage of Dendy Young (Dendy was a graduate of FDC and was mentored by Dan Young—no relation) and building DLT Solutions into a boutique powerhouse from the mid-1990s to the early 2000s. Focusing on SGI at Falcon showed Craig the value of developing a niche in the government market and also helped him to develop and hone a skill that was to become the envy of many in the industry.

Carahsoft describes itself as a "government IT solutions provider delivering best-of-breed hardware, software, and support solutions to federal, state and local government agencies. Formed by a group of seasoned professionals with decades of experience in government sales, government marketing and federal GSA contract management, Carahsoft has built our reputation as a customer-centric organization."

Several manufacturers knew Craig and his ability to focus on and develop programs around hot niches. Though he generally keeps a very low profile personally, his manufacturing partners and his company gain massive traction through very targeted outreach programs—programs that largely stayed off the radar of the rest of the market for the first few years. These programs were (and are) designed to educate the customer and begin the relationship-building process.

Using seasoned salespeople, a tightly focused marketing program, Craig's relationships with manufacturers in hot and emerging niches, and massive focus, Carahsoft began growing market share from the start. By 2006, Carahsoft was receiving industry awards regularly, less than three years after starting—so much for staying off the radar. By 2008, those awards included being ranked sixteenth on *Inc.* magazine's list of fastest grow- ing private companies, and in 2009, Carahsoft was one of the top 10 companies by total revenue on *Inc.* magazine's list of America's 500 fastest growing private companies.

In late May 2010, Carahsoft made it onto the top 100 fed- eral contractors list published by *Washington Technology*. Inside of seven years, Carahsoft was ranked ninety-ninth in Global One—doing business with the government. And this doesn't count the state and local government business Carahsoft also pursues. This is truly amazing growth.

I hesitated in using Carahsoft as an example because the model devised by Craig Abod is very difficult to replicate, especially in the now seven-year time frame since Carahsoft's launch. When he started the company, he had the reputa- tion, the relationships, the ability, and the knowledge. His ability to execute was displayed previously with SGI at Falcon and with DLT. The pieces of the puzzle were all there, and Craig's ability to put the pieces together for a third time is now very public.

One of the many reasons I decided to include Carahsoft is the mentor factor: Dan Young mentored Dendy at FDC; Dendy started Falcon Microsystems and mentored Craig. Each of them provide those around them the opportunity to watch what it takes to play and win at a very high level.

MANUFACTURER TO DISTRIBUTOR

For IT, the distributors include companies such as Ingram Micro, TechData, Arrow, and others. For office products, SP Richards is probably the biggest one.

The major role of the distributor is to help get products from the manufacturers to those that sell the products to their respective customers. Another role is to help provide product information to the resellers, information that helps them sell specific products or to specific markets. Some of the distributors have programs specifically for the government market. For example, Bob Laclede is the general manager for government programs at Ingram, and David Harris the director of government sales at SP Richards. Both are widely acknowledged experts in the government market and deservedly so.

Ingram Micro started the first major government program back in 1995 with Partnership America. Curt Cornell began the program shortly after he left Novell to join Ingram. He went to Ingram specifically to start this program. Ingram asked five companies that provided support and training to resellers to serve as advisors to the program. These advisory companies then helped the resellers that did not know much about the government market in starting the process. Partnership America had a law firm, a contracts specialist, two others, and the marketing guy. I was fortunate enough to be among the five companies asked to advise Ingram's reseller community.

Ingram's outreach to those interested in selling to the government included briefings, seminars, a newsletter, a special section of the early Web site, and more. While rarely providing anything earth shattering, Ingram did a major service for the reseller community by providing them with one source for valid and useful information. Then, as now, there were too many venues where one could get bad or questionable information.

PRIME TO SUB

Knowing how to subcontract is key for most companies trying to do business with the government. Most of the money the government spends is through larger contracts. Especially for those companies selling services, learning the subcontracting ropes is critical.

Several primes have small business outreach programs to facilitate this process. Ludmilla Parnell runs such a program for

General Dynamics Information Technology (GDIT). Among her many duties are industry outreach (you can find her every year at the OSDBU conference), reviewing the capabilities of small businesses seeking to subcontract with GDIT, and making introductions only when there is a really good fit.

SUB TO PRIME

Make no bones about it: The sub-to-prime relationship is a subordinate relationship. Your ability to help a prime is predicated on doing what is expected of you and more. When you identify an opportunity to get more work on their contract, take it to them, regardless of whether the work fits you, them, or another sub. The program manager will remember this. When you have added a skill to your repertoire that can add value to the contract, inform them. This is not always a two-way street, but it does allow you to build agency relationships as well. While you are busy working on one contract with the prime, always ask, when you can, who the other program managers are at that company.

COMPANY TO MEDIA

The value of good press relations is difficult to overstate. If you are mentioned in a positive way in one of the publications that serve your niche, you have an endorsement that cannot be bought: a validation and blessing from an industry insider. People who get quoted are automatically thought of as experts.

There is a vibrant government trade press, represented by publications such as *American City and County, Federal Computer Week, Federal Times, Governing, Government Computer News, Government Executive, Government Product News, Washington Technology*, and many others. See Appendix 2 for a more detailed list and for Web links.

Reaching out to press contacts can be done in many ways and is often as simple as picking up the phone and calling.

Having gotten more press than most in this market, at least as a consultant, I can honestly say that good relationships with editors and reporters are worth their weight in gold, but they are relationships that do not suffer abuse or subterfuge. When an editor or reporter calls me and asks me something about an area in which I have no true expertise, I will offer to introduce them to one of my expert friends who can answer the question much better than me. This simple act gives me more credibility with them than anything else I can do.

PEER TO PEER

The peer-to-peer relationship is your basic professional relationship, developed over time. Each of us has a network of some kind. This type of relationship is the kind we all have but few work hard at maintaining. You can't maintain relationships with hundreds of people on a one-on-one basis, but you can leverage social media (such as LinkedIn) to manage these relationships to an extent. We will discuss Web 2.0 tools in detail in Chapter 11.

VENUES FOR BUILDING RELATIONSHIPS

So, where do you begin your journey into building relationships in the government market? Start by thinking of the government not as one market but as a vast confederation of interrelated communities. Finding the right communities for your niche is the key.

Relationships can develop anywhere, but you really need to identify the key venues where you can strike gold early and often. We touched on this in Chapter 5, as networking in the government market is a huge part of marketing, sales, and business development.

PROFESSIONAL ASSOCIATIONS

Professional associations are always important. The government market is a major market segment, comprised of both vertical and horizontal markets. Too many people make the mistake of treating the government market as a vertical one, not seeing that it spans over transportation, banking, energy, health care, real estate, and more. This is germane here because in associations for transportation, energy, health care, and others, you will find key pockets of government influencers—the very people you need to know.

From the mid-1980s through the mid-1990s, I advised contractors on direct marketing to the government. A large part of that was direct mail, and there were some problems getting "commercial mail" distributed inside government agencies. During my research into the problem, I discovered a small community of mail professionals inside government agencies. They got together on a regular basis to share best practices on managing the flow of both incoming and outgoing mail.

The group, the Committee on Mail Policy (COMP), was open to meeting with industry representatives. John Long (then with *Federal Computer Week*) and I got some of the publications and larger mailers, such as GTSI, to join together to form the Association of Mailers to the Federal Government (AMFG; I wasn't great at coming up with an acronym that spelled something that sounded like a word). The AMFG met with members of the COMP on a monthly basis for over 18 months. While they were more concerned with outgoing mail (as the government is the largest mailer in the world), they did work with us to resolve certain problems regarding incoming mail.

We created a venue to network with those who directly influenced an area in which we needed some action. It still happens that way today. When you see an apparent void, fill it. If the void needed filling, others will show up.

Another venue for the GSA Schedule vendors is the Coalition for Government Procurement, a membership organization that represents GSA Schedule vendors on Capitol Hill and provides good education and networking.

So, aside from associations, where do you, as a C-level, need to network?

EVENTS

The option of what events you may attend is going to be largely dependent on what you sell and how you sell it. If you sell true commodity products on GSA, one venue that is critical is the annual GSA Expo. While this is attended by thousands, you can set some appointments ahead of time so that you can meet with key people while you are there. Find some brains to pick.

Good events remain great places to meet potential customers if you pick the right events. The first criterion for selecting events is how long the event has been going on. If it is truly a known and respected venue, you need to consider it.

The next event-selection criteria are the pedigrees of the producers. There are hundreds of events for the government market every week in the Washington, DC area, and many of these are produced by companies that have been around for only days or even hours. Several of these events, especially since 9/11, have been organized by paper companies, promising the most valuable networking ever but producing nothing after they deplete your funds. Unsuspecting companies fall for this all the time, especially those new to the market.

I saw one event announcement from a company I suspect of this that listed several high-ranking feds as speakers. I knew a couple of the people listed, so I called them and asked. They did not know of the event or the producer.

Often, you need tactical events to leverage some sales activities. These tactical events come in the form of agency-specific events, technology-specific events, or contract-specific events. In-agency tabletop expos fall under one part of agency-specific events. I have recommended these for years because they continue to produce. Sales can and do occur on the expo floor.

Technology-specific events are great if that is your arena. With these, you are able to network with other specialists, yet another subcommunity in the government ecosystem. The same is true for contract-specific events. I have attended many of these—most recently, the DHS Eagle event and the annual SEWP conference. The Eagle event had DHS buyers and influencers from all over the country and from each DHS component in attendance. I delivered the keynote address at the NASA SEWP contract conference in May 2009 in Austin, Texas. When I arrived at the hotel, the conference staffers were already mixing with the contractors and other agency buyers. It was like a family reunion.

YOUR TO-DO LIST

1. Start building your personal network—peers with whom you can compare notes.
2. If you are a novice, seek a recognized industry expert as a mentor.
3. You need to join and participate in one or two industry groups. Select them carefully, and don't be hesitant about swapping one out if it is not productive. Don't join a group if you don't plan to be active.
4. Cultivate relationships with a few key reporters or editors. If appropriate, invite them to your office.
5. Check the events your staff selects, and if you do not attend, have them debrief you shortly after the event. Keep your finger on the pulse.

CHAPTER 7

The Myth of the Level Playing Field

How Small Businesses Can Play

Over the past several years, the volume has risen from both sides of the political spectrum over how important, how great, and how necessary small business is—such a vital part of the U.S. economy! Fallout from that includes various small business initiatives in government policy regarding the availability of contracts to small businesses.

In reality, this has led to regulations and goals without teeth but with plenty of loopholes. Companies that are far from being small bid on and win set-aside contracts, sometimes because they used to be small and occasionally because they select an NAICS code under which they can bid as a small business.

As mentioned earlier, there are more than 560,000 companies registered to do business with the federal government through the CCR Web site (www.ccr.gov). The vast majority of these are small businesses. Many companies that register here think that the act of registering will lead to calls from government agencies or major contractors with lucrative offers. This does not happen. Just like companies that get a GSA Schedule thinking the phone will now ring, many small businesses think that if they announce their set-aside status, a contract will appear. This is the perpetual complaint of OSDBUs and the small business liaison officers at the prime contractors: someone walks in, announces their small business status, and expects a contract to appear.

For a small business to get any traction, real action must occur. There are skills that have to be in place first. Here is a story from Larry Allen, the president of the Coalition for Government Procurement (www.thecgp.org):

> SNVC is a small, veteran-owned business located in northern Virginia. Established in 1998, it was originally run by five experienced former military officers and civil servants. At the time, SNVC had the "know-what" needed to sell to the federal government, but not necessarily the "know-how." They were successful in establishing a base of federal business; but over time, they found it difficult to expand. Being small in a sea of larger businesses was tough going. Customer after customer told them, "We really like you, but you need to get a GSA Schedule contract."
>
> SNVC did just that. Two years after they were established, they sought help from specially trained GSA Schedule experts to help them understand both the business opportunities and responsibilities of holding a Schedules contract. With that outside help, they put together a strong Schedules offer and negotiated a contract with good pricing and with good terms and conditions.
>
> Next came growing their business. SNVC was smart and knew the value of relationships, so they continued to focus on the people and the market they

knew best. It was important that the team not try to be everything to all people. After all, they were still a very small company, and time had to be used wisely. Their Schedule contract provided a streamlined avenue for customers to reach them. Contracting challenges were minimized so that they could focus on delivering their "know-what" of their value proposition. It is important to note that they stressed their value proposition first. They did not rely on their small business size status. Size was not the first selling point that they used to generate business.

Consequently, SNVC's business escalated through the years, partially because they had a Schedule contract that allowed customers to reach them easily. During the first year, SNVC's annual revenue was $98,500. Today, they are on target to exceed $20 million. In 1998, SNVC's customer base consisted of two primary clients and five people.

Today, it is a respected entity comprised of nearly 100 professionals, all providing outstanding service throughout the Army sector of DoD and within DISA [the Defense Information Systems Agency]. To attain that kind of success, SNVC had to clearly compete with—and beat—larger businesses. SNVC's president has been quoted as saying, "Our GSA Schedule was critical to our business growth. It opened up doors both directly and indirectly for our firm."

It hasn't always been smooth sailing, but SNVC continues to sell its value proposition to the federal market every day. They realize that marketing their GSA Schedule is not something you do just one day and then watch what happens. Rather, they know that this has to happen every day. Having been a Schedule holder for 10 years now, they also know that compliance is critical, so they have invested in that, too. Doing so, the firm keeps as much of its revenue as it can.

SNVC continues to be an excellent example of what a company with the right value proposition and dedication to overall federal market success can be.

THE SMALL BUSINESS TWO-STEP

There is the Texas two-step, and then there is the small business two-step. The small business two-step goes like this: A company representative goes into a small business office (government or contractor) and announces his or her company's business status (SB, WOSB, SDB, VOSB, etc.); then, they wait expectantly for a contract to appear, like manna from heaven.

Whenever I interview a government small business officer (OSDBU), I ask what their main complaint is about companies coming in for their first agency visit. Invariably, they tell me that most companies come in with little preparation and almost no knowledge of what the agency does, and they open by giving their business status: small business, 8(a), veteran owned, HUBZone, and so on. Then, they want to know how to get a contract with that agency—preferably within the week.

The OSDBUs are advocates in their respective agencies for small business, but they have no control over contract awards. Their role for vendors is to educate companies on agency mission, products purchased, and methods used for purchase. Their role inside the agency is to help find qualified small businesses to assist the agency in fulfilling the mission, to make introductions when necessary to aid that process, and to remind all agency shareholders in the contracting process of the legally mandated small business requirements.

What the OSDBUs want companies that visit them to do is to define their area of expertise, match that with the agency mission and align it with current needs, and come into the office prepared to learn. Once a skill is matched with a need, traction can occur. And this is just the beginning. I have interviewed several OSDBUs on my radio show, *Amtower Off Center*, over the last three and a half years, and each one has the same message: Lead with what you do well. Don't tell me your business status; tell me what you do! Judy Bradt of Summit Insight (www.SummitInsight.com) offers a free download called "Make the Most of Your OSDBU Visit" under the "Resources" section of her Web site that is quite good.

Judy and I are among an ever-growing group of consultants that help companies enter the government market successfully. Check credentials before you hire one.

From a public perception viewpoint, it is in the government's best interest for people to believe that when Uncle Sam spends our tax dollars, he is doing so in an equitable manner—that any qualified company has an opportunity to bid on and win any given contract. While it is pleasant to think that this is accurate, it is not. It isn't even close.

While it is true that any qualified company may bid on any given opportunity, it is not necessarily true that they have the ability to win. The playing field is not level. The reason you are reading this book is to make certain you know how to play on a field that is not now, and never was, level.

There is a great deal of misinformation about small businesses and doing business with the federal government. The FAR 19.201 reads, "It is the policy of the government to provide maximum practicable opportunities in its acquisitions to small business . . . concerns. Such concerns must also have the maximum opportunity to participate as subcontractors . . ." The operative word here is "practicable," as it provides an out for any contracting officer who decides it is not practicable on a particular contract to include set-asides or who opts to off-load the set-aside component to the winning prime contractor(s).

So, what do you do to make certain you can get some business?

There are many things the total novice can and should do. As mentioned in Chapter 2 when we discussed contracts, it is critical to understand where you fit in the scheme of things. A big part of that involves understanding what your business status is, what it means, and what it does not mean.

BASIC SMALL BUSINESS PROGRAMS

We discussed the various types of small businesses in Chapter 3. They include small business as defined by the NAICS code you select, woman-owned small business, small disadvantaged business, small disadvantaged business 8(a) certified, historically underutilized business zone, veteran-owned small business, and service-disabled veteran-owned small business.

Each of these designations may allow you to bid on contracts that are open only to small businesses or contracts that are open to a subset of the small businesses just listed. Each also allows your company to claim this status if you have a GSA Schedule contract. The GSA e-Library even highlights business status. Many procurement officials who are buying commodity or other products and services from the GSA Schedule check the size status of the Schedule holder when making their decisions. Each of these, along with your technical area of expertise, may help you get on other bidding and contract-performing teams.

So much for the mechanics side of things. Now, how do you leverage any of this?

Here's how one small business positioned itself to win business.

LONG-TERM PLANNING PAYS OFF

Marissa Levin started Information Experts (www.Information Experts.com) in October 1995 from her kitchen table. Information Experts is a creative communications firm offering strategic and tactical communications services across digital and print media, with a focus on human capital continuity and improvement. For the first seven years, they focused exclusively on commercial work

Around 2002, she took a long look at some of the work the government was doing in her sweet spots: instructional design and curriculum development, human capital management, strategy consulting, marketing communications and outreach, and technology development. Looking at where some of her competitors were getting business, she found the Office of Personnel Management (OPM) Training and Management Assistance Office (TMA) and the two contracts they manage: one for human capital management and one for training. These contracts offer multiple services that are open to all federal agencies. These services include learning solutions (training program development), performance management, workforce productivity, business process reengineering, compensation system development, work and life programs, strategic workforce planning, and management strategies.

The two TMA contracts were a perfect fit for Information Experts, and they were just coming up for recompete. These contracts recompete on a five-year cycle. Marissa decided her company lacked the experience, the corporate infrastructure, and any credibility with the customer—including past performance and agency contacts—so she decided to pass on responding to the RFP.

Over the next few years, Marissa and key staffers researched the OPM TMA contracts. She went through the 8(a) certification process and obtained multiple GSA Schedules. She made several visits to the OPM to discuss aspects of the program with key agency personnel, making certain that over time, they knew her and her company. She filed a Freedom of Information Request (FOIR) for contract information and researched her competitors. Through these actions, Information Experts developed the corporate infrastructure, including financial systems and an RFP bid process. She used the RFP process to go after other government business in the interim.

The final important task undertaken by Marissa and senior staff at Information Experts was to evolve a winning strategy for the TMA contracts. Her total cash investment in pursuing the contracts was over $300,000, which is a lot of money for a small business—and that number does not necessarily include the hundreds of hours invested in all other facets of the research.

The results: When the draft RFP came out, all the pieces of the puzzle were in place for Marissa and her team. Information Experts was awarded a prime contract on both contracts. On one contract, there are 27 contractors, and on the other, there are 18. She still has to compete for business, but she now has another contract she can use to do this, and her team is good at that.

Now into her third year of the contract, she has expanded her work into over 15 government agencies. She is also bidding direct and teaming with others to continue her growth as a contractor.

One issue that is not readily apparent from this story but that is palpable to the government customers is Information Experts' employee retention rate. They maintain attrition below 10 percent, and many of her employees have been with her since the early days, now 10 or more years. This is the kind of stability the government loves.

Lessons learned: When she knew her company was not ready, she did not walk away. She knew, over the very long term, that Information Experts was a great fit for government work. She invested five years in pursuing the OPM TMA contracts but also developed other contractual vehicles (GSA and others) along the way. She pursued the 8(a) status and developed relationships with key OPM personnel. She studied the contracts and her competitors, and she positioned her company as a player—a player with past performance credit earned through the other contracts she was awarded over the intervening five years. Finally, she developed a winning strategy for the TMA contracts. In her own words, after all that, "not winning the contract(s) was not an option."

RESEARCH

No small business status guarantees you anything. As I have stated many times, this is a relationship-driven market. You must determine who you need to meet from the government, the industry, the press, the investment community—whatever it is going to take to get your company moving over the rough and unfamiliar terrain of the playing field.

In one of our interviews, Bob Davis offered the two-two-two method for the novice company. As a small business, you need to identify two prime contractors, two medium-sized businesses, and two agencies. Each of these targets is predicated on the value *you bring to them*. Match your skills with the prime contractors based on what contracts they have in place or are pursuing. Much of your research can be done at company Web sites and at government agency Web sites. Dig deep at the government sites and you can find some really useful stuff.

Let's address Bob's two-two-two. How do you determine which prime contractors are currently involved on contracts that cover your area of expertise or are likely to bid on emerging contracts? We will get deeper into defining your area of expertise in Chapter 8, but you need to know your area of expertise to do the research.

Select two prime contractors based on the contracts they currently have and on your ability to add value in a niche. Select two midtier contractors based on the same. Finally, select two agencies based on what they do (the mission) and what they need (where you fit).

Brad Antle, former CEO of SI-International (purchased by SERCO in early 2009), was a guest on my radio show after the sale of SI, which was then a midtier contractor (below $1 billion) and growing. It had a great contract-win rate and was gaining momentum. Brad said his ability to partner with key small businesses was a significant part of his growth plan. Finding small businesses that had hot areas of expertise and key relationships with agencies in place were absolutely critical in his win rate and overall growth.

Washington Technology (www.WashingtonTechnology.com) is one place to research the prime contractor community. *Washington Technology* is the major publication for the systems integrator/prime contractor, midtier contractor, and small business contractor communities. Regular features cover bid and proposal, merger and acquisition, hot contracts, procurement issues, and more. The *Washington Technology* top 100 contractor list provides some initial data that can help you narrow down your search for a potential prime. *Washington Technology* also publishes lists of contracts that should be on everyone's watch list.

Knowing where to find contract information short of using the Freedom of Information Act (FOIA) is important. Government spending can be tracked through www.usaspending.gov, but personally, I find that of limited use. All spending above $25,000 is supposed to be reported through the Federal Procurement Data System (FPDS; www.fpds.gov/fpdsng_cms). Here is what the Web site reports on its FAQs page:

> Agencies will report on all contract actions using appropriated funds as specified in FAR 4.6. AbilityOne (formerly JWOD Nonprofit Agency or Sheltered Workshop awards) and UNICOR (Federal Prison Industries) awards are reportable, as they are not interagency agreements.
>
> Below is a partial list of types of awards reportable to FPDS-NG [Next Generation]. See FAR 4.606 for the full list. Agencies will report unclassified information on all contract actions using appropriated funds including, but not limited to, those made:
>
> - with replenishable stock and revolving funds.
> - with appropriated funds transferred from one executive agency to another where the servicing agency contracts for the supplies or services.
> - with appropriated funds obligated pursuant to the provisions of PL [Public Law] 85-804.
> - by one agency to another.
> - for supplies and equipment.
> - for construction, alteration or maintenance of real property.

- for services, including research and development and utilities.
- AbilityOne (formerly JWOD Nonprofit Agency or Sheltered Workshop awards).
- telecommunications from regulated carriers; and
- Federal Prison Industries, i.e. UNICOR awards (orders from GSA stock for UNICOR products are not reportable).
- Agencies will report all contract actions made with funds held in trust accounts for foreign governments or procurements for foreign governments regardless of the nature of the funds. (The term "foreign governments" includes international organizations.)

As you can see, the FPDS could be a good place to start. Another tool is the FOIA. You can use the freedom of information form (available in the e-Reading room of every federal agency Web site) to request information. Fee-based services, such as Input, and Federal Sources also provide valuable information on who is bidding on emerging contracts, as well as strategic introductions. There are also many consulting firms in the Washington, DC area that help in this arena.

Scott Lewis of PS Partnerships is one such consultant with experience in getting companies in front of the right primes. Scott and others also train their clients on how to act, what to say, what the main points of the conversation should be, and more. However, just because he can introduce you to a prime does not mean he will. His access to key personnel at the prime level is predicated on not wasting their time. Scott's pedigree is pretty thorough: He has been an executive at Input and was publisher at *Washington Technology*.

There are many such experts available who can help, and you will meet many of them at the networking venues discussed next.

NETWORKING

Nothing replaces building relationships. In any market, there are multiple venues at which to network: seminars, briefings, lunches, associations, professional societies, and on and on. How do you make your initial determination on which of these is best for you? As you develop relationships with key people, ask them three questions:

- What do you read (trade publications, not the local newspaper)?
- What do you belong to?
- What do you attend?

These were questions I posed in my first book, *Government Marketing Best Practices*, and they remain valid today. What you are trying to find out is where people in your niche congregate to share ideas and meet other people.

The first place to look for networking opportunities is any event sponsored by federal or military agencies in your immediate vicinity. Military bases will host small business events, as will regional clusters of federal civilian agencies.

If you are in the Washington, DC area, there are a myriad of briefings, seminars, networking events, and the like where you can meet key people. Events sponsored by the IAC, TechAmerica, the Professional Services Council, the AFECA, and others are generally well attended. For small businesses, the ASBC is good.

For women- and minority-owned businesses, there are other networking venues that can be quite important. This is by no means the entire list of organizations. A few of the most popular for women include the following:

- Women in Technology (www.womenintechnology.org)
- Women Impacting Public Policy (www.wipp.org)

- National Association of Women Business Owners (www
  .nawbo.org)

For minorities, there are these:

- National Minority Business Council, Inc. (www.nmbc
  .org/home.html)
- International Entrepreneurs (http://dc.tie.org)
- U.S. Hispanic Chamber of Commerce (www.ushcc.com)

Another networking venue that has become a significant factor in the Washington market is Mark Bisnow's extraordinary e-media powerhouse (www.bisnow.com). Mark popped up on my radar during the dot-com era as the public relations guru for one of the bigger start-ups, MicroStrategy. He became, among other things, a radio talk show host and occasionally broadcast his show from the main dining room of the Tower Club in Vienna, Virginia.

After the dot-com era, he dropped off my radar briefly; then, around 2005, the first Bisnow e-newsletters showed up. Among the publications is *FedTech Bisnow*, which actually has a national focus. Short, pithy, and full of photos, it offers a *People* magazine–style view of the government market, with a focus on the DC environs. It covers IT-related events, visits various company offices for profiles, and includes an occasional "Where Are They Now?" feature. Here is their description from the Web site:

> *Bisnow* is a *vast media empire*. At the moment, the aforementioned empire mainly consists of *twelve e-newsletters* focused on business niches in Atlanta, Boston, Chicago, Dallas-Fort Worth, Houston, Los Angeles, New York and Washington, DC. But we also do lots of events, since they usually involve *food* and often drink. The Bisnow schtick is to be colorful,

entertaining, picture-heavy, yet informative and fluff-free. We also try to make reading quick: short copy, bolded words. The amazing upshot? *People actually read us.*

In 2009, Bisnow began hosting events, which became instant hits. These include industry briefings and pure networking opportunities. To ensure attendance, the event registration lists are often used as part of the promotion, and they often read like a who's who.

If you attend, look up the always scruffy-looking Dave Stegon, the official photographer and editor of *FedTech*. See if he'll take your picture for the next edition of the publication. Each time I've been in it, I get e-mails within hours saying, "Hey, just saw you on Bisnow!"

Bisnow's tagline, "Bisnow: (almost) Never Boring" is dead-on accurate. In homage, when I recorded my first radio show at the Tower Club, Mark was my first guest.

Research again will be key for you in finding the right venues to meet, learn, and identify your sweet spot in the market. Keep in mind these lessons from Marissa Levin and Information Experts: Target an opportunity, research everything about it, visit the agency and get to know them and let them get to know you, put your infrastructure in order, don't be afraid to spend some money during the process (making certain you have checked the credentials of those you are spending your money with), and execute well.

YOUR TO-DO LIST

1. Find some good advisors.
2. Conduct agency research via the Web and with multiple site visits.

3. Start creating a must-read list of publications, including e-news.
4. Find networking venues and attend. Encourage your employees to attend. Get debriefed on each to determine which could be best; you cannot go to them all.
5. Develop an internal information-sharing forum for your company. Let everyone share what they find.
6. Add www.GovEvents.com to the sites you review for educational and networking venues.

CHAPTER 8
Differentiation Is the Key

"They really need this (name of product/service here)*! There's nothing like it anywhere else!"* It never ceases to amaze and amuse me when I speak with someone who has a "truly unique" product or service, something earth shattering that the government needs and will want immediately. Calls and e-mails like this come in on a regular basis—not just to me, but to many of the consultants with whom I network.

There are several things wrong with this scenario, the first of which is that if the product or service is that new, the likelihood is that it has no "commercial viability"—no track record. The government wants products and services that have been tested elsewhere. When the government has a unique requirement, they put out RFIs and RFPs *after* they define what they need.

So, in the world of government contracting, how do you stand out—stand apart from your competition? Since day one, there has always been more than one provider for every product and service the government buys. There is always someone right behind you, waiting to sign up. The more crowded your niche or category becomes, the more important it becomes to stand out from the crowd. Jack Trout and Al Ries established the idea of differentiation in *Positioning: The Battle for Your Mind* (1981). David Meerman Scott moves the theory of positioning to Web 2.0 in his best-selling book *The New Rules of Marketing and PR* (2007); I recommend reading the revised second edition (2010).

So, how do you do stand out in a crowded market that is allegedly driven by lowest cost?

DEFINING YOUR TURF

In the early 1990s, a group of women in the IT sector got together to start the association Women in Technology (WIT; www.WomenInTechnology.org). I was the only male at the organizational meeting, which proved to be a major differentiator in multiple ways. Suffice it to say I was there because I thought it was a great idea and wanted to show support. Needless to say, I stood out. At that meeting, I met some extraordinary women, including the one who became the first WIT president, Valerie Perlowitz. She also became and remains a good friend.

At that time, Valerie had her own company, Reliable Integration Services, and she was one of a handful of women entrepreneurs who had established her own businesses focusing on government. This was before the federal goal of setting aside 5 percent of contracts for women-owned businesses, an issue that Valerie actively supported at the federal and state (Virginia) level.

Reliable Integration Services focused on one area of the IT market: networks. This was an area that most IT firms claimed some expertise in, in the mode of, "Oh, yeah, we can do that, too." However, Reliable claimed it as their sole area of focus and expertise. Even after the women-owned businesses became recognized for a set-aside goal, the Reliable Integration Services Web site proudly proclaimed on its home page, "Networks: Nothing but Networks" in big, bold letters. Unless you already knew, it was not easy to find out that the company was a woman-owned business. Reliable led with its technical strength.

In a seemingly mundane area of the vast IT market, Reliable Integration Services managed to carve out a niche by choosing as a focal point their true area of expertise—and it was an area of expertise that resonated with the two major audiences Valerie needed it to resonate with: government techies and systems integrators.

TRUTH IN LABELING

Regardless of size, many IT companies find it necessary to label themselves as "systems integrators," a term those in the federal market apply to the top tier of contractors that pursue the massive contracts. Companies such as General Dynamics IT (GDIT), Lockheed Martin, SAIC, Boeing, Northrop Grumman, Raytheon, and others occupy the vaunted role of systems integrators. These huge firms are much more service oriented than product oriented, looking to solve the myriad of issues facing the government in the technology arena. For these companies, size is often the apparent differentiator. But you will also find that the areas of expertise come in the form of the agencies and programs they focus on.

This is also why both Dell and Hewlett-Packard purchased companies that provided services. Dell bought Perot Systems, and Hewlett-Packard purchased EDS. Both companies wanted to migrate into the systems integrator and services side of the business. Further, this is why mergers and acquisitions continue in the government market at a pace higher than outside the government market: Size dictates the ability to go after larger contracts.

When a small vendor claims the systems integrator status, it is generally done so because the company believes it has a better chance of winning business if they cast a broad net, claiming they can do it all. This strategy does not work in the government market, simply because small vendors cannot scale themselves to the tasks that status implies. In some instances, it also marks the company as a rank amateur. How can a 10-person company be a systems integrator?

The tactic employed by Reliable Integration Services is the best way to differentiate in the government market. Most companies have some sort of core technical strength— something they do well. This is the natural competitive advantage each company has, to greater or lesser degrees. Reliable took their strength in networks to the extreme: This is what we do; it is all we do. The result was that they got business directly from government agencies and through subcontracting opportunities.

Reliable differentiated by identifying an area that was not necessarily hot, but it was certainly necessary, and the need was ongoing. They became very good at it and as a consequence became well known for it.

You can also differentiate by identifying an emerging need and helping to bring it to fruition.

DIFFERENTIATION IN HOW YOU DO IT

How about differentiation in a mundane services area such as maintenance? Ralph W. "Pete" Peters is the founder and president of the Maintenance Excellence Institute, and he is a true cheerleader for the maintenance industry. The Web site address for his membership organization is www.pride-in-maintenance .com. Pride in your work is a differentiator everywhere.

Pride is part of how you do something. So, how can you leverage a process to become a differentiator?

From 2003 to 2005, I consulted with CDW-G, the government-facing unit of CDW. I began following CDW in the early 1990s. From the time I started my business, I was fascinated by the companies doing business primarily through catalogs, and I sought ways to bring them into the government market. I still find catalogs fun to work with.

During one of my early visits to the Chicago-area CDW headquarters, I was given a tour of the warehouse by the president of the government division, Jim Shanks. He was involved in the design of the computer system used in the warehouse and was justifiably quite proud of it. The total layout and design allowed CDW and CDW-G to offer same-day shipping, with order accuracy that was high above industry standards. It was an amazing tour and a really cool warehouse. Having worked with several catalog companies at that point, I had been in more than a few warehouses. The United Parcel Service had dedicated loading docks at the CDW warehouse, with the big trucks waiting at 2 PM.

My major observation to Jim that day was that the warehouse afforded CDW and CDW-G their first major differentiator in the government market for IT products: same-day shipping. Up to that point, no major government contractor, especially the biggie—GTSI—could make that claim or anything close to it.

This became an early cornerstone in the CDW-G message to the government: If you need it quickly, call us.

I was so enamored of the warehouse operation that I obtained permission that fall to schedule a tour of the warehouse for CEOs from other B2B catalogers who attended my annual summit on selling products to the government. I did not go on the tour, as there were other attendees at the summit, so I asked catalog industry guru Don Libey to act as my liaison. When the CEOs returned from the tour, they were at least as impressed as I had been, and I could see their wheels turning: How can I use some of this in my warehouse? Even Don Libey, who is not easily impressed, was in awe of the warehouse. Industry gurus don't get excited too easily, as they usually have seen much of what is at or near the edge.

For CDW-G (and CDW), this was, and remains, a powerful differentiator. It is very easy to overlook the most obvious differentiators if you don't know what will truly resonate with your prospective audience. Those in the catalog business took it for granted. Heck, for years, B2B office-supply cataloger

Viking Office Products had its president and founder, Irwin Helford, on its catalog cover, touting next-day delivery. People in the industry assumed everyone did this.

Government contractors, though, were not direct marketers and were accustomed to a much slower fulfillment process. And for government buyers, the concept of next-day delivery was truly awesome.

The message resonated with government buyers and CDW-G began to grow, all because of a very simple differentiator—one taken for granted in the trade.

SEGMENTATION

Here's another lesson from the catalog world and their reliance on reading the data. From the mid-1980s through the late 1990s, there were many companies selling computer products through catalogs, and several of these found the government an attractive market. The federal credit card (then the IMPAC card, now the SmartPay card) made the government market lucrative for the computer catalogs. Among the leaders in this niche were CDW, PC Connection, PC Mall, Tiger Direct, PC Compleat, and others, including the direct sellers Dell, Gateway, and Micron PC. At one time, I was tracking more than 20 B2B and B2C computer catalogs; CDW was always among the top I was monitoring.

In the late 1990s, CDW did something very different— something that put them at the top of my watch list and made them a company I was interested in advising. Through customer analysis conducted by in-house database guru Bill Singleton (then with CDW, now with Allant), they identified several vertical customer clusters, one of which was the public sector. They took that data and created a separate catalog they called *CDW E&G* (for education and government). Shortly thereafter, they further segmented education and government into separate catalogs. The result was market share growth in each segment.

The major difference in the catalogs was the cover: *CDW-Government* and *CDW-Education*. I am certain there were some different products emphasized for each market, but the simple act of recognizing that the markets viewed themselves as having different needs and addressing that concern with different catalogs proved to be a winner.

Within a few years, CDW-G was basically a separate entity targeting all of the public sector, including education and federal, state, and local government. As a result, more growth occurred in each niche they targeted with a different catalog. They differentiated by providing each market segment with a catalog exclusively designed for that segment.

Regardless of the niche you are in—with a seemingly mundane product or service—differentiators can be found and leveraged. The caveat is that you have to understand the nuances of this market before you can determine what your true differentiators are.

These can vary from market to market, and no differentiator lasts forever. They morph as the market changes and as your competitors adopt your style, and you have to know when this occurs and adjust accordingly.

But what is the best way to determine what resonates with your niche in the government market?

Ask. It is that simple. Find some customers, or legitimate prospects, and ask them what matters most to them regarding the vendors in your product or service category. Do not prompt them by giving them a list; just ask what is different or better about the vendors they choose to buy from.

The more you are in the pure commodity category, the more you will find answers like speed of delivery, accuracy of orders, breadth of products offered, and customer service. When you get into higher-end products and more sophisticated services, you will find answers like responsiveness to inquiries, ability to troubleshoot and resolve problems, and the account representative's ability to understand what the customer needs to accomplish and the ability to help complete that task.

Sometimes, these are not easy to enunciate in marketing materials, but you can develop white papers, podcasts, and other information delivery tools that make this clear.

DEFINING, CLAIMING, AND DEFENDING YOUR INTELLECTUAL REAL ESTATE

But what is your area in the realm of ideas? If your area of expertise is more on the intellectual plane, there are multiple ways to define and differentiate. This could involve training in multiple disciplines, management consulting, organizational behavior, all types of research and development, and lots of other things described in the MOBIS (consulting services) arena of the GSA Schedule (Schedule 874).

If you provide management consulting services to industry, the likelihood is that the government buys the same type of service from someone. If you truly have a reputation and expertise in a specific area, this can translate into government business.

Whether you call it thought leadership or being a niche master or subject matter expert, it boils down to the same thing: You own some intellectual real estate; you have some claim to some knowledge that you and others find valuable. Intellectual real estate is that which will separate you from your competitors and help you stand out in an increasingly competitive environment.

Being a subject matter expert in a vacuum does not lead to business. In order to use this intellectual real estate to expand both your influence and your knowledge base, there are several things you need to do.

First, you need to define the niche you claim as your own, preferably in terms the government uses. Remember that the language here is different, and using the vernacular is important. It is usually better to define a narrow niche rather than a broad one.

What competitive advantage have you developed that differentiates you and/or your company from others in your niche? Define this in sufficient detail and in several ways. This can include developing a niche within a niche. For example, if you are a cyber security expert but your niche is information assurance (IA), then you need to lead with your IA credentials and experience. You can even take one of the components of IA (confidentiality, integrity, authentication, availability, or nonrepudiation) and make that your area of expertise. Be careful not to make the niche so narrow that those who need the service see it as a limitation rather than a true skill.

Second, establish your ownership claim on this niche. This claim should include education and experience, professional affiliations and accreditation, articles and white papers, speaking engagements, press quotes, blogging, and whatever else you have. Remember, owning intellectual real estate is never exclusive, and it is not a passive activity. It requires you to be active and constantly growing, adding value to the niche on a regular basis.

Diane Griffin of Security First Associates (www.Security FirstAssociates.com) did this by writing two e-books: *ISP Certification*, which is a manual, and *Everything You Need to Know about the Security Clearance Process, but Are Afraid to Ask*. Books, even e-books, further your claim to be a subject matter expert.

Third, incorporate this niche ownership claim into all of your collateral material, both online and offline. This includes using your LinkedIn and other online profiles as collateral. If you are establishing an area of expertise for a company instead of an individual, you need to carefully manage how each individual employee's profile is worded at the various social-networking sites. Provide a template with the proper wording for each employee to use for online profiles when describing the company and its areas of expertise. Use the keywords and phrases for your niche in all collateral material. There must be a unified front—a message consistent with the company's expertise that is sent out from each employee. If each employee has leeway to create his or her own message, the area of expertise can become vague.

Fourth, blogging almost becomes mandatory at this point. If you have an area of expertise, you must create venues in which to share at least some of your knowledge to foster interest and to create buzz about you as a focal point. Well-written blogs packed with solid information can become niche magnets. When you direct the appropriate traffic to them, blogs become online destinations where others in your niche will begin to congregate and comment. Once started, the blog must be regularly stoked, like a fire, to keep people interested. Posting at least on a weekly basis would be good. If you don't have anything new to add, write about something in the news related to your niche or books about your discipline—but post weekly.

Have multiple people contribute to the blog so that one personality or point of view does not obscure the subject matter. A good name for the blog, preferably something to do with the niche, can also drive traffic. Think back to Reliable Integration. One logical direction for Reliable could have taken them from networks (their message in the early 1990s) to government network security, an area that has become very hot recently. A blog or microsite with that name could be a good traffic driver for e-books, blogs, or white papers.

If you use a blog or microsite to drive traffic, you should also consider using an industry phrase in the name of the site's URL. You can research to see what URLs are immediately available by using Web sites such as Afternic, available at www.afternic.com. Think of Afternic as the eBay for URLs. When I visit, there are always a variety of technical names and lots of government-related URLs available.

Fifth, tie each of the activities together. Each online presence representing your company—the company Web site, LinkedIn profile(s), Twitter account(s), blogs, podcasts, and any other activities—should be linked. If the LinkedIn logo is included on a company's Web site, it is an indication that profiles of key employees of that company can be found at LinkedIn. Twitter's "Follow Us on Twitter" logo is also showing up everywhere.

Sixth, as previously stated, owning intellectual real estate is never exclusive, and you will always have competitors. While it is not necessary to mention them directly in any of your activities, if you are commenting on ideas originated by them, an acknowledgment must be made. This does not diminish your role but increases the trust the overall niche will have in you. Being a true thought leader requires acknowledging the legitimate contributions of each person in the niche.

Keep in mind that owning a piece of intellectual real estate is not a passive activity. Online marketing guru David Meerman Scott (author of the best-selling book *The New Rules of Marketing and PR*) blogs only twice a week or so, but he is pretty active on Twitter and Facebook. David opts not to use LinkedIn, and when I asked him about it, he explained that if he tried to do too many things, he would not do them well. It is better to be more active in a few key venues than a little active in many.

Seventh, make certain you create and maintain active relationships with many of those in your niche. This will include customers, competitors, journalists, associations, and event producers—anyone who has a vested interest and a venue. It will also directly involve key government players in your niche. The relationships we discussed in Chapter 6 remain pervasive in every facet of doing business with the government. In this instance, the relationships are with all of the influencers within your niche. The more you network with those in your niche, the more likely you will find the networking venues that pay major dividends.

For businesses, the online destination for networking is LinkedIn, and I suggest that you connect with as many people as possible in your network here. It augments but does not replace face-to-face networking. Always remember that this is a relationship-driven market. We will discuss LinkedIn in more detail in Chapter 11.

If you aspire to be a thought leader, to own some intellectual real estate, understand that the process is neither passive nor exclusive. It requires you to actively grow and share your knowledge base, to acknowledge the contributions of others, and to add value to this niche. It also means that you have to keep your finger on the pulse and understand when the niche is morphing and/or creating new subsets. Further, it keeps you in the center of the activity in that niche, and when that topic comes up, it is likely that you or your company will be discussed.

What was once a niche may now be a major category. The generic computer security arena has generated many subsets over the years, and each of those has led to others. Remember, keep your finger on the pulse and evolve with your niche. In the government market, that also means to follow the funding. Just because something gets lip service does not necessarily mean there is funding available for it.

Caveat: If you are not a true subject matter expert, this will fail in a very big way. You must be able to walk the talk.

COMPETITIVE ADVANTAGE VERSUS SUSTAINABLE COMPETITIVE ADVANTAGE

When government business development guru Bob Davis is pursuing a large contract, he looks at it this way: If the scope of the contract requires multiple disciplines or several different areas of technical expertise, you must find companies that offer these disciplines and then partner with them. Systems integrators are often looking for experts in various disciplines when a contract demands a specific skill. It is easier to be found when you have a reputation for a specific skill. Here, we are talking about the skill a company possesses, not the skill of an individual—unless, of course, that individual is a one-person company with an extraordinary skill set.

This goes back to the notion described earlier, but Bob looks at it with a slightly more discerning eye, the eye of a BD professional looking for subcontractors, teaming partners— those he needs to build a winning team for a contract. He wants the best for his bid team.

For him, a competitive advantage is something a company does well, probably better than 75 to 80 percent of the companies claiming a similar or overlapping expertise. Like the area of networking for Reliable Integration Services, it is something they lead with and do well. When you develop this expertise and demonstrate it with government clients and others in the government market through subcontracting and other activities, the word gets around.

During our discussions, Bob takes this concept to another level: the level of sustainable competitive advantage. Given that a competitive advantage is something you do better than 75 to 80 percent of the companies out there, the next level has to be something that differentiates you even further. To have a sustainable competitive advantage, you need expertise in a skill that you perform better than 95 percent of those offering the same or similar service. Moreover, this expertise has to be verifiable in the market—by past performance, testimonials, or other demonstrable methods.

Both the competitive advantage and the sustainable competitive advantage must resonate in the market. If you possess a skill far beyond any competitor but it is not a skill currently needed, you have to develop a new skill or find a market where that skill is needed. By the same measure, if you are too far ahead of the curve—an expert in an area that is new— the government may not yet be ready for or interested in your expertise.

Working with the government market successfully means staying current on what the government wants and how they want it, making certain you define your niche accordingly, being able to find the right companies to work with and to sell them on working with you, and finding the government customers who really want and need what you have, then convincing them that yours is the right company for the job.

Differentiation helps this to happen.

YOUR TO-DO LIST

1. What strengths does your company possess? Define these in terms that will resonate within the market.
2. Determine which agencies will most likely be interested in these strengths.
3. How are you communicating this skill set to those who want and need what you have?
4. Are you on the right contracts for those prospects?
5. Are you monitoring this niche to understand how it is evolving? Is it ready to divide into new categories? If so, what direction will you be taking?
6. Is there available agency funding for what you do?

CHAPTER 9

Execution

For our purposes, I define *execution* as focusing on completing the immediate tasks at hand and performing each of them well; doing everything you can to develop a beachhead in an agency. Many of those who have helped me over the years have said that focusing on one or two agencies that are a good fit for you, determining their needs, understanding how they buy, recognizing the internal agency issues and how those impact buying decisions—these and more are what execution is about.

The reason to focus on one or two agencies at a time is so that you don't spread yourself too thin. It affords you the opportunity to learn how to develop broader agency relationships after you have started your work, and it helps you to develop the critical past performance factors.

Being able to execute also means knowing what assets and skills with which you have to work within your company; taking inventories of both should be a regular practice. Your assets may be physical or intellectual property.

These assets and skills include technical and management skills, technical expertise, client relationships, contract support, new technology, intellectual property, or perhaps other processes that your company has developed. Knowing what these are and where they are in your company should assist you in the execution of current projects.

In an e-book I published with the help of several members of my government brain trust was a joint contribution from Robert Silverman of ReachSolutions and Steve Charles of immixGroup: *"The question you need to answer when determining your potential government market opportunity is not whether there is a market for your products and services, but precisely where in the government is your greatest market opportunity."* That "where" is how you decide the agencies on which to focus. (You will see more of this e-book in Appendix 3.)

Many seasoned government professionals have also stated that success in the government market is predicated on finding a process that works, a successful practice to replicate, a repeatable process. When you win some business, one of the first things you need to do is to analyze *how* you won it. It did not just fall into your lap. A quick initial win can hurt as much as help if you do not recognize it at once for what it was: a right-place, right-time coincidence. But there were probably other factors that you will overlook or forget to consider if you wait too long to reflect on how you won. With each win, you are looking to build a repeatable process. There are steps involved that you can replicate.

This is not the only process that needs mapping. For example, BD master Bob Davis has a checklist for the BD process that can include the following:

- General information gathering
- Attendance *and* visible participation at a key conference on behalf of a client
- Competitive information gathering that directly affects the decision to bid or not to bid a deal
- Generation and delivery of a specified (management, technical, or marketing) white paper on behalf of a

client developed by the client's small and medium-sized enterprises

- Senior executive meeting(s) with the client's senior management (i.e., nontechnical meeting[s])
- Secure a decision to bid a deal
- Join a leading bid team
- Support a Red Team review, who is the team pursuing a contract at the final stages before the award
- Support a Black Hat session, which is a team of people kept separate from your proposal response team who develop the technical solution and pricing usually for a specific competitor(s)
- Successfully submit a bid to the client
- Win a deal: GWAC, MAC, RFP, RFQ, or a task order (TO)
- BD review of existing projects to identify new business opportunities
- Development and execution of a postward sales plan

Bob's lists are rarely short, and they are always the result of hard-earned experience and extensive studying. While all of these activities may not apply to your situation, it may be a good starting list.

Execution also means making certain the details are properly addressed, such as being sure that all your contracts are compliant and that your staff is cognizant of any and all new rules impacting those contracts. It means ensuring that the relationships that help grow your business are in place and flourishing and that you and your staff are studying the market to understand if your niche is trending hot or cold and are deciding where the next sweet spot is going to be.

Execution also means keeping your staff as informed as possible on where the corporate bus is heading. The more they know, the more they can help. This is where companies with higher employee retention rates really start to pull away from competitors.

In an interview with Bill Hoover of American Systems (Federal News Radio, June 1, 2009), Bill said that retention of his BD staff made his company much more competitive. Clients and prospects inside government agencies appreciated the fact that American Systems BD staff did not change nearly as often as some others. Retention is transparent to the client. Part of your execution should be developing a corporate culture that supports and encourages employee retention.

Above all, execution means focusing on the winnable business at hand, developing a beachhead, and growing that beachhead into a front. If this sounds like war, that's because it is. You are not here alone. If you are visible in the government market, someone is watching what you are doing. They are watching to learn how you do it and to see if you make a mistake or misstep. Then, they will attempt to replace you. Marissa Levin watched the OPM TMA situation for several years before she was ready to go in.

Another example of winning the business in front of you comes from the experience of Micron PC (MPC). In the mid-1990s, I advised MPC over a two-year period. I was fortunate to work with a great team, which included Harry B. Heisler, Ron Clevenger, Ross Ely, and Tony Colangelo. At that time, MPC's direct competitors were Dell and Gateway. Rather than compete head-on with these much better-funded companies, MPC focused on growing business at the five agencies where they had the strongest relationships. As a result, they were able to grow their government business substantially by maximizing the value of each of those agencies.

I have heard on several occasions of instances in which a small business goes the extra mile during the bidding process to help the prime land the contract. After a loss, the small business might believe that it is the end of that relationship. However, in many instances, the prime knows and sees what the small business is doing. They are looking for subcontractors willing to put forth the extra effort, and they will look for you when your area of expertise is needed for another contract. It is the relationship that counts here, and with the small business working hard, even in a losing battle, the relationship is solidified. It is companies like this that you want on your team.

Execution may be something as simple as evaluating all of your systems, including credit card processing. Knowing that the government is migrating toward Level III processing is important for several reasons, the first being that it is written into some contracts. Level III provides the lowest transaction processing rate. But, in order to qualify for the lowest rate, Level III transactions must be passed through the processing system with much more detailed transaction information that Level I or II transactions. The next reason is that credit card processors are not created equally. Many of us had our processing system set up by our bank; this will rarely land you the best processing rate. Regardless of the volume of transactions you run, selecting a processor is critical for saving that extra half- or full point in processing fees. I have included a link to a white paper issued by FTS at my Web site (www.GovernmentMarketMaster.com) that outlines what you should look for in terms of a processor and fees, not to mention the security issues involved.

If you think credit card processing is mundane and not worth the effort, think of all the money the government spends via SmartPay, and then think of the margins you have and the GSA Industrial Funding Fee.

Here is another story from the 1990s to wrap up the concept of execution. CompUSA entered the government market in the early 1990s. The small DC-area office was under the leadership of Bill Griffin, with a team that included Frank Araby, Jim Connal, and Randy Jacobs, and marketing advice from guru Bob Gosselin. They ramped up a program primarily through GSA sales that was grossing about $120 million a year, competing head-on with the major government reseller GTSI.

Things went well until someone at the corporate level (in Texas) decided that everyone should be under one roof. They recalled the team—but the team opted to stay in DC and migrate, with their relationships, to other contractors. I am still in touch with all of them. While Bill has retired to points south, Bob, Jim, Randy, and Frank are still in the government market and are all doing well.

While the DC-based CompUSA team executed very well, the company, in effect, executed the team. CompUSA continued doing business with the government, but their growth rates stagnated. Without the team in place in DC, the critical relationship factor was gone.

YOUR TO-DO LIST

1. Do you have one list of all the things your company is doing right now? If not, how long will it take you to make the list?
2. Every time your company does something well, map the process. Reverse engineer everything that went on and map it out.
3. Create an inventory of your skills and assets. Update this at least twice a year.
4. Develop a way to share information internally and make it an active discussion.
5. Map your employee retention rate and find ways to improve it.
6. When something is working well, don't change it unless it can be improved.

CHAPTER 10

Building Momentum

While execution means taking care of the things already on the table, building momentum means expanding your arena incrementally as your capabilities and knowledge grow.

Building momentum means many things in the government market, but it especially means knowing where you fit at any given moment. It involves feeling the nuances and understanding when those nuances are evolving. Although it moves slowly, the government market does change. Focus on your niche, and make certain you and your company are evolving with it. Execution is what Marissa Levin did over the five-year period she was targeting the OPM TMA contracts—five years of preparation leading up to the RFP and contract win.

MARKET INTELLIGENCE

Market intelligence plays a big role in momentum. The intelligence should come from formal and informal sources and should be shared internally. Formal sources can include market research that you commission from Input, Federal Sources, or Market Connections. Market Connections of Fairfax, Virginia, conducts an annual survey of the buying habits of federal managers for IT. This tracks the movement of how they gather information for purchasing decisions.

Having seen the results of this survey for several years, I have observed the migration from offline sources of information to online sources of information. I have also witnessed this firsthand and have written extensively about it for the last 15 years. Understanding how key government buyers and influencers are getting information should influence how you provide it to them.

Building momentum in the government market depends on many factors, starting with your feet on the street—your people who meet with government clients and business partners. The feet on the street provide informal market research. One of the constant themes in this book is the relationship factor, and momentum is built by creating, maintaining, and learning from as many useful relationships as possible. Each of these relationships has to work both ways. If you want to add value to a relationship, which is the only way it will last, you have to bring something to the party.

The relationships (see Chapter 6 for more details on relationships) needed include peer-to-peer industry relationships, client (government) relationships, those developed in various trade groups and associations, those with key members of the press, those in the investment community, and occasionally those developed with politicians who are more directly concerned with the operations of government—anyone who can influence your position in the market. This is not to say that you have to develop and maintain all of these relationships yourself, but along with your key staff members, these relationships are crucial to keeping your momentum going.

In 2001, I brought together a few trusted colleagues and introduced the concept of starting a monthly educational and networking forum. Along with David Powell of the Federal Business Council, Joan Daly of Daly Associates, and Lisa Dezzutti of Market Connections, we held our first government marketing forum in August 2001 and attracted about

50 people, which is excellent for a summer event. Although we had to cancel our forum scheduled for September 12 of that year, we built momentum beginning with the October event. One reason for starting the forum was to create a venue for government marketing professionals, a group that was not separately served at that time.

One of the regular attendees of the forum was Guy Timberlake. At that time, Guy was a BD manager for a small IT services firm, but he had some ideas of his own. In late 2002 or early 2003, Guy ran his idea by me. He wanted to start an organization to help small business gain real traction in the government market.

Over the next several months, we spoke many times about this. He was getting feedback and advice from multiple sources, and in 2004, he started the American Small Business Coalition (www.theasbc.org). With relatively modest membership fees, the ASBC began gaining some traction by adding real value to small businesses, earning the trust of small business advocates inside the government, and acting as a facilitator, not a consultant, to the relationship-building process. Momentum increased as the word spread organically through press and radio interviews and through adding value to the community.

This occurred because Guy worked hard for his members, got several of them involved in helping to manage meetings, and put together a board of advisors that met regularly and assisted Guy and his wife and business partner, Margaret ("Maggie"), in creating a direction and refining it along the way. I was the first chairman of the ASBC board and served on the board for four and a half years. As of May 2010, the ASBC had 542 members. These members represent 32 U.S. states and four countries outside the United States. Since the group began, ASBC members have been awarded over $3 billion in government contracts.

When I was serving as chairman of the board of advisors to the ASBC, I met some really great small business CEOs. One who stood out early on was Jae Collins of Prime Solutions. Founded in 2003, Prime Solutions focuses on government work primarily as a subcontractor. The following is a frontline lesson from Jae.

LEMONS TO LEMONADE: GRACE UNDER PRESSURE

My parents had certain phrases they used to try to motivate me or assist in my emotional recovery as a teenager. One of those phrases was the adage "Make lemonade out of lemons." Thankfully, as I aged, that small cliché remained inside my mind for resurrection and implementation.

Fast-forward several decades. A company I started with a colleague, Prime Solutions was on the precipice of its first "big" (this is a relative term) government sub-contract recompete. It comprised more than 50 percent of the company personnel, it was the genesis contract for the company, and it was where my partner got his start in the government. The government was combining two contracts into one (we were the bigger of the two contracts).

As the pre-RFP dance began, it seemed like we had everything lined up. We had intimate knowledge of the client and the ear of the capture manager. While our incumbent contractor stumbled in the midyears of the contract, it seemed they had righted the ship in the final 18 to 24 months. We had critical assets strung across several technical task orders (TTOs).

The first warning sign came when all our strategic input for the proposal was deleted. The second came when the government broke the one-stop-shopping principal of contracting and asked for more detailed information from both parties. Our prime mistakenly thought that their limited response requirement was a better sign than the competitor's more detailed response requirement.

In the end, the government selected the competitor prime:

- The smaller of the contracts
- The higher-priced proposal
- The lesser-known organization

At first, a cold chill ran through our organization. We only had four other subcontracts, which were sparsely funded and not offering a lot of openings. Also, this was the beginning of the software engineer gold rush, and our employees were getting offers from everyone and their brother.

The saying "United we stand, divided we fall" was never more relevant than at this moment. I gathered the employees affected and conveyed to them that they must not give their resume to any company on the winning team, else my leverage with the winning prime was gone. It took an eye-to-eye meeting with each employee and a direct request for them to give us 30 days of trust and faith.

Our second step was to secure a meeting with the prime. This is difficult after a contract award, as they are franticly trying to meet with the client for transition talks, meet with their teammates to determine deliverable people, and ramp up their own program office. We were successful in securing the meeting, but it took most of the 30 days.

Our final step was to show the prime the challenges they would face during the transition and how we could assist them. With each statement, we focused on how we could ease their pain and not on the fears of our own critical dilemma.

In the end, we were one of two incumbent companies added to the new team. In two years, we tripled our contract size. Success is not determined in intervals but in the end. As long as you are armed with a keen mind, perseverance, and a juicer, options abound.

When the wheels fall off the bus, either put them back on or get on the next bus. Jae caught the next bus. His ticket was Prime Solutions' past performance and agency connections.

CEO VISIBILITY AND ACTIVITY

When you reach a certain level, to maintain the momentum, you have to become more active and more visible in your niche. This involves activities across many venues outside the normal running of a business. Your active participation in various industry groups and events becomes a must, even if they are focused exclusively in your niche.

Let me emphasize that last part a little more. Your niche is where you make money. It consists of the government agency or agencies that use what you do, the other players in that niche, and the publications, Web sites, and so on, that serve that niche. One of your jobs as you build momentum is to be more pervasive in your niche—to develop the reputation of a player in that field. This does not happen of its own volition; it is something at which you must work.

It especially involves understanding as many of the niche nuances as possible, including granular things such as whether there is an intra- or intergovernmental group of people in that niche that is not visible to the naked eye. The Committee on Mail Policy was such a group when I worked with them in the late 1980s in trying to resolve mail delivery issues at federal agencies. If you are involved public key infrastructure (PKI) issues, knowing that there is a PKI working group might be of interest. There are many such groups throughout the government; not knowing about them is not an option if you want to maintain momentum and have an edge on your competitors.

Ardell Fleeson has been a major player in the C-level networking arena for two decades. While she is not a C-level, many know her from her various roles in the community, the main one of which is networker extraordinaire. When I met her, she was the membership director of the Tower Club in Vienna, Virginia. Just about everyone in the government contracting community in Washington, DC, is familiar with the Tower Club. To explain what the Tower Club is to prospective members, Ardell would simply say, "Power breakfasts, power lunch." When prodded, she would explain that at each table, there was always a potential deal occurring. I have been a member since the mid-1990s and served a term on the board of governors.

Every time I would go, Ardell would introduce me to someone. One time, it was Brian Roberts, the CEO of a small IT shop called CroixConnect. Brian and I struck up a conversation, which eventually evolved into a friendship. It also got me on his radio show twice—and drove me to get my own show.

Now, why would the CEO of a small company want to host a time-consuming radio show?

Brian's company could not afford a top-level BD professional to go out and seek the relationships he needed to take CroixConnect to the next level. So, he thought about the issue: How do I meet key people in the companies I want to do business with, and how can I get on their radar? The answer came to him in his car: Why not host a radio show? You can buy unused airtime on many stations and host your own show.

If Brian called the CEO of a $500 million corporation to pitch his company, he probably wouldn't get through. But if he called as the host of his local business talk show *Taking Care of Business with Brian Roberts*, he could probably get the attention of the right people.

Brian's program aired Saturday mornings on a DC talk radio station, and he was able to record shows with several key executives in the government market, as well as other national business figures. Through one contact he made after an interview with a CEO, CroixConnect landed on a contract that he had targeted.

The radio gig may not work for everyone, but it is a great example of thinking outside the box. Fortunately, Brian was a very good talker and an excellent talk show host.

THE CHANGING LANDSCAPE

The election cycles can impact some government programs, and you must be aware of those shifts if any of the programs you are working on may be impacted. Over the past few election cycles, both parties have claimed to be the friend of small business, but when it comes to government contracting, it is all lip service, regardless of the party in power. Be leery of politicians who are seeking votes on the small business platform. Very few members of Congress understand the difficulty small business has with conforming to the regulation-laden process of doing business with Uncle Sam.

Although the government market seems to move slowly, the movement under the surface can change things quickly. You don't want to be caught off guard. There are always factors at play that can undermine what you are doing: political interference in the form of earmarks or other congressional intrusion, funds being redirected by new agency priorities, court rulings impacting various set-aside programs (these are happening more frequently), and so on.

Building momentum requires being able to shift at a moment's notice. I was at a seminar recently, and the speaker was explaining how he and his partner got their first big break. They were meeting with an intelligence contracting official about some potential IT work the agency was going to bid. But before they could bid it, they needed a secure facility setup ASAP. One of the partners had experience in that area from his time in uniform, and the intelligence contracting officer probably knew that. The upshot was that they built the sensitive compartmented information facility (SCIF) and won the IT work. Now, their company operates in both areas, and both are doing well.

When the goose lays a golden egg in front of you, it may want you to pick it up. When a contracting officer explains a need to you in some detail, they are looking for help.

If you are aware of the potential shifts in the market and prepare for them accordingly, you will be in a better position than 90 percent of your competitors.

YOUR TO-DO LIST

1. Develop sources for gathering market intelligence, both paid and free.
2. Attend events where you can meet key people.
3. If the wheels fall off the bus (contract), see if you can get on the winning contract.
4. Consider creating venues where you can meet key people. Think outside the box.
5. Pay attention to elections, especially the presidential elections, and monitor how they may impact your current contracts or contracts that you are tracking.

CHAPTER II

The Missing Link

Web 2.0 Tools

Web 2.0 represents a sea change in marketing. While Web 2.0 is simply a set of tools, it is a set of tools that allows us to interact in ways not even the great science-fiction television shows or movies could have imagined. The Jetsons may have been closer.

My personal advisor on all things Web, Amy Africa, CEO of Eight by Eight, keeps pushing me to incorporate more of these tools into my marketing. And David Meerman Scott, Web 2.0 guru and all-around great guy, notices when I am blogging more often. I do use certain Web 2.0 tools, as you will see, but I do not spend an equal amount of time on each.

What exactly is Web 2.0, and what are the tools? According to Wikipedia, Web 2.0 is "commonly associated with Web applications that facilitate interactive information sharing, interoperability, [and] user-centered design." For the purposes of our discussion, we will address social networks, Twitter, podcasts, webinars and distance learning, Web radio, wikis, blogs, and video.[*]

---

[*] Source: http://en.wikipedia.org/wiki/Collective_intelligence

In late 2003, I began receiving e-mail invitations to join something called LinkedIn. I had no clue as to what this was, but the invitations kept coming. They were from people I knew but not really well.

LINKEDIN

Then, a couple came from people I knew better—people who would not be wasting their time on something superfluous. Frank Araby, who I had known for over 10 years at that point, was one of those people. Frank is a talented sales guy, so he is not going to spend his time spinning his tires on some Web site that does not pay him a dividend.

So, on February 11, 2004, I joined LinkedIn. I was an early adopter but not an early adapter. I sat and waited for something to happen. I reached out to a few people and waited some more. It wasn't until I read David Meerman Scott's *The New Rules of Marketing and PR* about three years later that I became fully cognizant of the power and reach of social networking. Of the nearly seven years I have now been on LinkedIn, over two were nearly dormant. Then, I took off.

I mention the dormant stage because that's where most people find themselves after signing up for social networks. They get pinged quite often to join, so they join. Then, they do little or nothing. The title of Jason Alba's book describes a question most of us have asked ourselves: *I'm on LinkedIn: Now What?* That little book made Jason an instant star and sought-after speaker. It also put his publisher, Mitchell Levy of Happy About, on the map. The book was a "print on demand" book from Happy About (www.HappyAbout.com) and it took off, largely because of word of mouth via social networks.

So, what does this have to do with you? This could be an entire book on its own, but here's what is has to do with those of us in the little niche called B2G, or as I prefer to call it, Global One. As I write this in late May 2010, there are almost

70 million business professionals on LinkedIn, over half from the United States. By the time this is published, I am predicting LinkedIn will be pushing 100 million members.

The entire *Fortune* 500 is here, and as near as I can tell, all of the top-tier government contractors are here as well—the executives and the frontline folks. There are also thousands upon thousands of federal, state, and local government employees on LinkedIn. As of late May 2010, there were 4,072 groups on LinkedIn that had something to do with the topic of government, and there were a total of 617,755 groups. Every time I check this, the number grows. I manage several groups under the Government Market Master banner, targeting niches in the government market.

While the membership count at LinkedIn may seem like a paltry total next to that of Facebook, remember that I qualified LinkedIn by saying that it is inhabited by business professionals. This is a network designed for business professionals, not one that is being retrofitted to adapt to them. Nobody wants to "write on my wall" at LinkedIn. Ultimately, they want to connect, share ideas, and do business.

While social networking is not face-to-face networking, it really is the next best thing. It allows you to find potential partners, prospects, and employees, and it helps you identify others in companies or agencies you may not know. It provides you with a venue to manage the network of people you know (by inviting them to connect) and to expand that network by reaching out to others with similar interests. It can, and does, lead to face-to-face networking as well.

Look at it another way. How many business cards do you collect at any given networking function? Have a couple hundred lying around in drawers? Every time I meet someone I want to stay in touch with, if I get their card (or even just their name), when I return to my office, I immediately reach out to them through LinkedIn (and 90-plus percent are there) to add them to my network. Instead of sending out the prewritten invitation provided by LinkedIn, I send a personal note, reminding them that we met at the networking event, and invite them to connect. I don't send invitations to everyone I meet, but I do send them to those I think I can help or who may be able to help me.

In one of my *Washington Technology* columns, I discussed the value of LinkedIn for connecting with the top contractors. The article, "Top 100 Tips: How Social Media Can Connect You to the Market's Biggest Players," was posted on the publication's Web site (www.WashingtonTechnology .com) on January 10, 2010. Very shortly thereafter, I had a significant spike in invitations to connect on LinkedIn. Key people in the market are there.

Why did they reach out? In the article, I outlined my plan to connect with those on *Washington Technology*'s list of top 100 contractors. Whereas once I sat down with the publication, a highlighter, and a note pad to make a list of the people I needed to meet, I now could sit down at my computer and open the *Washington Technology* top 100 list on one screen and my LinkedIn account on another—and start matching the top 100 companies with my connections, building an outreach program that would ultimately allow me to connect with each of the top companies in the market.

As a result, the people who wanted to connect with me were doing so to shortcut the process of themselves connecting with the top 100. If they were connected to me, perhaps they could use me to reach the bigger fish. That article remained all week on *Washington Technology*'s list of the top five most read articles.

IT marketing consultant Fred Diamond has been an occasional guest on my radio show, *Amtower Off Center*, on Federal News Radio (1500 AM in Washington, DC). Fred was once a client, back in the early 1990s, when he worked for Apple and Compaq, but he opened his own company, Diamond Marketing, several years back. On his first visit to the show, he told me about a small contractor client he was advising. Because the client had a solution that was a tight fit for three different contracts, he or she needed to reach the prime contractors on those three.

Fred instructed the client to identify the companies on LinkedIn, make contact through their connections, and try to set up meetings. Within two weeks, connections had been made with all three contractors, and meetings for each had been scheduled.

LinkedIn offers a number of good applications that you can add to your profile as well. These include the Amazon .com reading list to share what you are reading, a Twitter link to display your "tweets," a TripIt application to show your travel schedule, a Box.net feature to store your online files, a Google presentations application to post a PowerPoint presentation, an events application to announce upcoming events, a Blog Link feature that displays the headlines from your latest blog post, an application used to issue polls (if you wish to conduct a survey), and more. LinkedIn is aggressive in adding features and is working hard to be a vital business tool—and it is succeeding.

If your company is not approaching social networking in a focused way, developing an overall strategy, and using the necessary tactics to meet the strategic goals, you are falling behind quickly. Developing a social media strategy is no longer an option for any company. You need to develop a plan; if you are unsure how, seek some help.

LinkedIn is just one piece of the Web 2.0 puzzle. There are other social networks and Web 2.0 tools: podcasts, webinars, Web radio, wikis, blogs, and more. Where do they fit?

OTHER ONLINE SOCIAL NETWORKS

While I did seem to brush aside *Facebook*, it is not quite that simple. Facebook does have thousands of businesspeople and government employees as members. It also has thousands of groups for these people to join if they so choose. However, the problem is that they are mixed in with everything else that is there. One size does not fit all, and I don't see Facebook as being a top contender in the B2B or B2G market. All that being said, I do (barely) maintain a Government Market Master group on Facebook.

In some respects, Facebook is easier to use than LinkedIn for communicating with those you are connected with, and it also contains tools for posting events, starting groups, and the like.

GovLoop (www.govloop.com) was started by Steve Ressler when he was a fed. It was designed to be "by, for, and about govies," and as I write this in late spring 2010, it just broke 30,000 members. While small by comparison, it is all government, all the time. There are good discussion forums and lots of interesting members. GovLoop also maintains groups on LinkedIn and Facebook.

The *Federal Contractor Network* (TFCN; www.tfcn.us) is what its name implies: an online network for contractors. I am not certain if it began on LinkedIn or Facebook, but it maintains groups at each. Founded by Alex George, TFCN seems to be gaining strength by soliciting content from key members.

Both GovLoop and TFCN are built on the Ning platform, which allows anyone to start a community.

You should take a careful look at each of these before deciding where to focus, because I certainly do not recommend focusing on all of them. As I mentioned, I have joined all of these, but my social networking focus is LinkedIn. Join as many as you like, but focus on one or two.

THE WEB 2.0 TOOLBOX

Twitter seems to have taken the world by storm. In early 2010, I kept hearing that it was the hottest of the hot, with thousands signing up each day. While it has gained some traction in the government market, it appears mainly to be useful for sharing news or telling people what session you are attending at the conference de jour. While I realize this is an unfair characterization, I don't see this iteration of the platform as being a long-term play—but I've been wrong before.

Yes, I am on Twitter (@amtower), but I do not tweet regularly, nor do I read tweets regularly. I am still trying to figure out the value proposition of being too connected.

As yet, I see no reason why a small contracting company needs to join Twitter, with the possible exception of wanting to "follow" someone whose attention you seek. You can use Twitter to follow, then possibly connect with, that person.

There are several key Twitterers in the government market, and these will be posted online at my Web site (www .GovernmentMarketMaster.com).

Podcasts and Web Radio

Podcasts are audio white papers, or at least that is how I view them in relation to business. They are designed to be from 8 to 12 minutes long, although some are longer and some shorter. They are also supposed to focus on a single topic. You can listen to them at your computer, or you can download them to your portable device of choice.

There are several reasons to use podcasts for business. The first is to provide information about your company and area of expertise, and the second, immediately following that, is to provide that information in as many ways as you can. If you publish white papers only as pdf files, you are going to miss reaching those who prefer to listen as opposed to read. Some may prefer to download the audio files and listen to them while driving, during daily walks, or when jogging.

Keep them short and focused. When planned and executed properly with a good voice behind the microphone, podcasts are a valuable tool in your Web 2.0 arsenal.

Other audio formats include *Web radio* (also called Internet radio or streaming audio), which has come of age. I have been a guest on several Web radio shows over the past four years or so, and they have ranged from very well done to really bad. This format is not for everyone, as radio is not as simple as it may appear. To be successful, a show needs a talented host who can draw good information out of both good and bad guests.

From my perspective, a good talk show should be similar to a good conversation. The host, though, must primarily ask questions and let the guest shine. The host needs to keep a good flow going, so having a number of agreed-upon topics ahead of time is beneficial.

A Web radio show can help solidify your position as a player in your niche by using your ability to attract other key players. You could become the default audio outlet for any given niche in the government market. If you do this well, you can gain significant traction.

Adriel Hampton, a public servant in San Francisco, founded *Gov 2.0 Radio*, a Web radio show on the Blog Talk Radio network (http://gov20radio.com). Needless to say, it focuses on the government's use of Web 2.0 tools, and in my opinion, it is a good show. Adriel's cohosts are Steve Ressler (yes, the GovLoop guy!) and Steve Lunceford, a consultant at Deloitte. The lineup of these three makes *Gov 2.0 Radio* a hot spot for the Web 2.0 community.

Another good Web radio host is Jon W. Hansen, host of the *PI Window on Business*. Jon is a Canadian consultant and speaker and uses the show to display his many talents.

The station that airs my show, Federal News Radio in Washington, DC, has some great Web 2.0 features. Several of the station hosts blog at the station Web site (www .FederalNewsRadio.com), and all of the shows are archived for replay and download. They are also simulcast so that you can play them from your computer. Many of the hosts also tweet, as do many from most media platforms.

Remember this about Web or terrestrial radio: The shows always need guests. If you are not going to host your own show, consider approaching any show germane to your market (including local shows) about being a guest. If you have a decent personality and provide some good insight, you may be invited back.

Distance Learning and Webinars

The idea of *distance learning* has overcome many obstacles to become a leading method for online education. Online universities such as Capella University and American Public University (both fully accredited) offer courses only online. A major component of distance learning for the contractor community is the use of *webinars*. Cisco has invested lots of money in the WebEx platform and has purchased other online learning platforms to enhance what they believe will be a rapidly growing opportunity.

Many of the most successful companies in the market rely on webinars and other forms of distance learning to reach and teach prospects about various technologies, tools, and products. They do not want to sell, but to educate. These tools are great for prospecting and retaining customers. Some of the faster-growing companies such as Carahsoft and DLT Solutions host lots of webinars with their manufacturers for both prospecting and customer education. Cisco literally has a library full of webinar content for each of the markets it serves, including the government.

The next generation of these platforms incorporates video and more into the equation. Companies such as KZO Innovations (www.KZOInnovations.com) are really on the bleeding edge of this.

The next time you receive an invitation to a webinar, accept it—not because it is on a topic in which you are interested but because it is an opportunity to see for yourself how webinars work and to think of ways in which you might be able to use them in your business.

There are multiple platforms from which to choose to host your company's webinar and distance learning sessions, such as Citrix's GoToMeeting platform, Cisco's WebEx, and others.

If you are shopping for a platform, check out KZO Innovations, too. The technology around webinars and distance learning is a rapidly evolving and expanding area. It is also critical for you to understand how it can fit into your marketing, sales, and BD processes.

Wikis and Blogs

According to Wikipedia, *wikis* are "typically powered by wiki software and are often used to create collaborative Web sites, to power community Web sites, for personal note taking, in corporate intranets, and in knowledge management systems." Wikis are another way to share and collaborate.

Blogging allows you to post your thoughts and seek comments from those interested. Debbie Weil wrote perhaps the first important book on *blogging* for businesses titled *The Corporate Blogging Book*. Blogs may serve as valuable tools for thought leaders; on the other hand, they can be used by someone who wishes to prove the theory about the infinite number of monkeys with typewriters.

Done well, and publicized properly, a blog can create a community around a niche. Chris Dorobek's blog, the *Dorobek Insider*, is popular, as Chris is a well-known radio host and Twitterer. He is always interviewing interesting people and posting links to the audio on his blog. He has the integration of the Web 2.0 platforms working well. Mashable (www.Mashable.com) also features bloggers facing the government market.

Many of those in the media blog as well as tweet. Most of the editors and reporters that I know do both, and they do them better than many—especially the blogging part. They know how to stay on topic.

There are several niche blogs in the federal market, each attracting some portion of the traffic available for its respective niche. Many companies have corporate blogs as well. It is important to be sure that these are well written and remain on topic.

And if you don't want to write your own blog, you can stay in the game by commenting on other people's blogs. Identify the main blogs for your niche, monitor them until you see a topic where you can add legitimate value, and then go for it.

Video

The final Web 2.0 tool we'll look at is *video*. If you are a speaker, this is powerful. Have someone record you while serving on an expert panel or giving a presentation, and then post the video on YouTube. While there are not yet thousands of good examples out there for the contracting community, there are certainly enough examples from other markets to give you some ideas.

Like any other visual platform, video affords you an opportunity to register ideas to your target audience through visual imagery. Done well, this could be a strong addition to your arsenal.

LINKING THEM ALL TOGETHER

When you use these tools, publicize them. LinkedIn and the other social networks allow you to post your other accounts. If you are a blogger, you need to have your LinkedIn, Facebook, and Twitter links available right from your blog.

Every time I write an article, one of the things I do is post a link to it on all the pertinent group pages on LinkedIn and direct traffic to it. I also include as part of my LinkedIn profile that I am a contributor to various publications, so I am able to add the article to my profile as well.

Web 2.0 is where the world is heading, and apparently, Web 3.0 is not far behind. Take a hard look at these tools. If you have younger people on your staff, ask them for their thoughts on how these tools might be leveraged to help your company stand out in the crowd.

The best ideas are going to come from those who grew up in a wired world.

YOUR TO-DO LIST

1. If you are not yet a member, join LinkedIn. It is free. Then, look me up.
2. Make certain your LinkedIn profile is 100 percent complete. It will tell you when you get there.
3. Look at the other social networks, Facebook, GovLoop, and TFCN. Join each, but determine which is the best use of your limited time.
4. Sign up for a webinar and decide how you can use this platform for your business.
5. Start reading blogs. Buy Debbie Weil's book if you want some coaching on blogging.
6. Audio is important. Consider podcasting or even a Web radio show.
7. Look for pertinent video for your niche and consider how you might incorporate this into your outreach program.
8. Sign up for a Twitter account and follow others. Find a list of the gov-Twitterers at www.GovernmentMarket Master.com.

CHAPTER 12

Final Thoughts on Staying on Top of the Game and Becoming a Government Market Master

One size does not fit all, but everything we have discussed thus far can help you master your niche. Each path to success in this market will differ from others, even others that are successful in the same niche.

Success will be dependent on your staff—your ability to bring them up to speed on the nuances of selling to the government market or to hire key people with the necessary government experience and get them to fit in your company.

Your success will be dependent on your ability to set up the infrastructure necessary to pursue and win government business.

Staying on top of the game will mean something different for each company, and it means something different in each niche. It is dependent on company size, company goals, current and targeted contracts, and more. It also depends on whether you are growing your business to keep or to sell. Government Market Master Dick Stieglitz, author of *Taming the Dragons of Change*, can advise you in either scenario, but he will tell you that it is better to know early which way you are going.

Taming the Dragons of Change is an excellent book for C-levels. It is a collection of short vignettes written by Stieglitz detailing how he started and ran his government contracting firm, which he eventually sold. Each vignette has a lesson learned, often the hard way. His second book, *Expensive Mistakes When Buying & Selling Companies . . . and How to Avoid Them in Your Deal*, deals with the process of selling a company. This is another book to add to your library, as mergers and acquisitions in the government market are constant.

Coming into the government market means that sooner or later, if you are successful, someone will make an offer. When you begin winning business, you appear on someone's radar. What will you do when that happens?

Staying on top of the game also depends on whether you wish to remain a niche player or to develop multiple areas of expertise. I would strongly suggest that you always look to expand your skill set predicated on where the market is heading. Many of the small companies I have watched over the years have added skills incrementally, often at the request of the agency they are working with. However, many of these add-ons become profit centers beyond that initial engagement.

It depends on whether you will use your own money or investment funds to grow your business, and it depends on employing an organic growth strategy as opposed to growth by acquisition.

But staying on top, like building momentum, is predicated on having all cylinders running smoothly, and when they are not, fixing them quickly.

Becoming a top-level CEO and a Government Market Master will mean many things, but any leader needs to be able to clearly communicate with his or her employees. Writing is a skill most of us think we possess, but in fact, most are poor writers. The same applies to speaking.

Speaking opportunities emerge for many CEOs, but return engagements are often harder to come by. Why? It is because too many people heard you the first time. Speaking in a boardroom or to a small gathering is not the same as serving on a panel at a conference or even presenting a lunch or keynote address.

When I was working with Micron PC, they became the principle sponsor for a new conference, GovTechNet, which was a joint effort by *Federal Computer Week* and the Armed Forces Communications and Electronics Association (AFCEA). Part of their sponsorship deal was an agreement that the CEO got to deliver the keynote. When I asked about his speaking abilities, I was assured that he was up to the task.

He was not, but mercifully, there were not many in attendance for the keynote.

Similar to what we discussed about hosting a radio show, the ability to communicate verbally is not a given. Training is required, and C-levels need this training for speaking engagements and interviews. Larry Tracy's book, *The Shortcut to Persuasive Presentations*, is a good resource. Larry and some other National Speaker Association members are also speaking coaches.

Communicating with your staff is always a two-way street for those who wish to excel in this market. Picking up news from the front lines and sharing it internally helps to keep everyone informed. It also encourages others to share any tidbits that may help fill in the blanks on some industry gossip that is pertinent to your business. The picture, hopefully, becomes clearer.

You become a Government Market Master by determining the niche you best fit in, then maximizing your presence in that niche. It doesn't always mean that you will be the dominant player, but it means that you have created a way to become a significant player in your niche.

By now, you should have a few thoughts on the types of people you may need to be around on a regular basis. Since the mid-1990s, I have maintained an inner circle of professionals

I can call on for just about any aspect of the government market. While this inner circle expands and contracts on occasion, it is still comprised of many I consider to be among the best.

These are the people I have as guests on my radio show, the ones I recommend to my clients and the press, but I also call on each occasionally to provide me with guidance, introductions, and industry news.

You need such a group: Perhaps industry peers with whom you can share, or maybe some industry veterans who can help in specific areas. What you probably need is a little of both.

But being a Government Market Master ultimately means understanding that you cannot know it all. You can master a facet of the market and then find others who can complement the weaker areas. When you can, hire these people. If you can't hire them, add them as advisors.

While there are several illustrative stories in this book, let's take one last look at Information Experts and Marissa Levin. While she knew her company was a good fit for the TMA contract at OPM, she realized that there were pieces of the puzzle missing. So, she did not bid. In the intervening *five years*, she put all the pieces together.

There are many lessons to be learned from Marissa's story (and hopefully this book), but the big one is this: This market requires time, effort, and sweat equity.

Be prepared to be in it for the long haul.

YOUR TO-DO LIST

1. Review the other to-do lists throughout this book again.
2. Communicate with your staff.
3. Identify any weaknesses and deal with them.
4. Develop an inner circle. Create a regular venue for meeting with them.
5. Consider getting some training for public speaking.
6. Enjoy the ride. This is the biggest market in the world.
7. Stay current by monitoring www.GovernmentMarket Master.com and the other web sites I mentioned.

Glossary of Common Government Terms

I have compiled these terms from a variety of government Web sites over a long period of time. The gov-speak for most is intact. While this is not a complete glossary, it is quite thorough and perhaps the most detailed I have yet to see.

8(a): See **Certified 8(a) Firm.**

Acceptance: The act of accepting by an authorized representative; an indication of a willingness to pay; the assumption of a legal obligation by a party to the terms and conditions of a contract.

Acquisition: The act of acquiring goods and services (including construction) for the use of a governmental activity through purchase, rent, or lease. Includes the establishment of needs, description of requirements, selection of procurement method, selection of sources, solicitation of procurement, solicitation for offers, award of contract, financing, contraction administration, and related functions.

Acquisition Plan (AP): An administrative tool in which agency program offices report their upcoming formal contract actions. It is designed to assist the program and procurement offices in planning effective and efficient accomplishments of an assigned procurement.

Acquisition Planning: The process by which the efforts of all personnel responsible for a procurement are coordinated and integrated through a comprehensive plan for fulfilling an agency's needs in a timely manner and at a reasonable cost. It includes developing an overall acquisition strategy for managing the acquisition plan.

Addendum: An addition or supplement to a document (e.g., items or information added to a procurement document).

Administrative Change: A unilateral contract change, in writing, that does not affect the significant rights of the parties (e.g., a change in the paying office or the appropriate data).

Advertise: To make a public announcement of the intent to purchase goods, services, or construction with the intention of increasing the response and enlarging the competition. The announcement must conform to the legal requirements imposed by established laws, rules, policies, and procedures to inform the public.

Affiliates: Business concerns, organizations, or individuals that control each other or that are controlled by a third party. Control may include shared management or ownership; common use of facilities, equipment, and employees; or family interest.

Agency: Any executive department, government corporation, government-controlled corporation, or other establishment in the executive branch of the government.

Agreement: A duly executed and legally binding contract; the act of agreeing.

Alternate Response: A substitute response; an intentional substantive variation to a basic provision or clause of a solicitation by a vendor.

Amendment/Change Order: A written modification to a contract or purchase order or other agreements.

Anti-Deficiency Act: Prohibits authorizing or incurring obligations or expenditures in excess of amounts appropriated by Congress and apportioned by the Office of Management and Budget (OMB).

Appropriation:　Sum of money from public funds set aside for a specific purpose.

ARO:　After receipt of order.

Assignment of Claims:　This is done through the Information Technology Solutions Shop (ITSS) when the payment address needs to be changed to a financial institution. It is stored electronically and goes to finance for fund certification after the contracting officer (CO) makes changes. The two components of this are (1) notice of assignment and (2) instrument of assignment.

Assistance:　A relationship between a federal agency and a contractor/recipient, the principal purpose of which is the transfer of money, property, services, or anything of value to a contractor/recipient in order to accomplish a public purpose of support or stimulation authorized by federal statute rather than of acquisition by purchase or lease of property or services for the direct benefit or use of the federal government.

Award:　Any instrument, signed by a contracting officer (CO), that provides government funds or other resources to an offer or that permits expenditure of such government funds or the use of such government resources.

Best and Final Offer (BAFO):　For negotiated procurements, a contractor's final offer following the conclusion of discussions.

Best Value:　The expected outcome of an acquisition that, in the government's estimation, provides the greatest overall benefit in response to a requirement; a term applied to comparing proposals and ranking them from best to worst, not only on price but on all factors stated in the solicitation.

Bill of Lading:　A written receipt or contract, given by a carrier, showing a list of goods delivered to it for transportation. The *straight bill of lading* is a contract that provides for direct shipment to a consignee. The *order bill of lading* is negotiable; it enables a shipper to collect for a shipment before it reaches its destination (this is done by sending the original bill of lading with a draft drawn on the consignee through a bank). When the consignee receives the lading indicating that payment has been made, the lading will be surrendered to the carrier's agent, and the carrier will then ship the goods to the consignee, and the bill of lading will be surrendered to the carrier. Note: Shippers frequently consign shipments to themselves on order bills of lading so that delivery is made only upon the shipper's order; the person or firm to be notified upon arrival of the shipment at destination must be designated.

Blanket Order: A contract under which a vendor agrees to provide goods or services on a purchase-on-demand basis. The contract generally establishes prices, terms, conditions, and the period covered (no quantities are specified); shipments are to be made as required by the purchaser.

Brand Name Description: A purchase description that identifies a product by its brand name and model or part number, or other appropriate terminology by which the product is offered for sale.

"Brand Name or Equal" Specification: A specification that uses one or more manufacturers' brand names or catalog numbers to describe the standards of quality, performance, and other characteristics needed to meet the requirements of a solicitation and provide for the submission of equivalent products.

Broker: A business that carries no inventory and has no written ongoing agreement with any manufacturer or manufacturer's authorized distributor to sell the products of the manufacturer.

Budgeting: The process of translating approved expenditures into funding allocations for a specified period of time.

Business: A contractor, subcontractor, supplier, consultant, or provider of technical, administrative, or physical services organized as a sole proprietorship, partnership, association, corporation, or other entity formed for the purpose of doing business for profit.

Business Information Centers (BICs): One-stop loca-
tions for information, education, and training designed to help
entrepreneurs start, operate, and grow their businesses. The
centers provide free on-site counseling, training courses, and
workshops and have resources for addressing a broad variety of
business start-up and development issues.

Certificate of Competency: A certificate issued by the Small
Business Administration (SBA) stating that the holder is "responsible" (in terms of capability, competency, capacity, credit, integrity, perseverance, and tenacity) for the purpose of receiving and
performing a specific government contract.

Certified 8(a) Firm: A firm owned and operated by
socially and economically disadvantaged individuals and eligible to receive federal contracts under the Small Business
Administration's (SBA) 8(a) Business Development Program.

CFR: Code of Federal Regulations.

Change Order: Unilateral written change order issued to
a contractor to modify contractual requirements within the
general scope of the contract. Such modifications are limited
to changes to the drawings, designs, specifications, method of
shipment or packing, or place of delivery.

Commercial and Government Entity (CAGE) Code:
A five-character ID number used extensively within the federal government. The Defense Logistics Information Service
(DLIS), who administers the CAGE code system, has a CAGE
code search feature on the Internet (available at www.bpn.gov/
bincs/begin_search.asp) that will help you determine whether
a code has been previously assigned to your organization. For
those not listed in the database, the CAGE code request process is incorporated into the Central Contractor Registration
(CCR) process. Therefore, your company will be assigned a
CAGE code during the processing of your registration.

Commercial Market Representation: A Small Business
Administration (SBA) representative who reviews and rates the
small business, small disadvantaged business, and women-owned

business subcontracting programs of major prime contractors and makes recommendations for improvement.

Commitment: The reserving of funds for obligation at the time the contract is signed by an agency's warranted contracting officer (CO).

Commodity: A transportable article of trade or commerce that can be bartered or sold.

Commodity/Service Contract: Previously referred to as "M-contracts." Since the inception of the Minnesota Accounting and Procurement System (MAPS), the contract number is a six-digit number assigned by the computer system. An "M" number is no longer assigned for these types of contracts.

Competition: A procurement strategy where more than one contractor that is capable of performing the contract is solicited to submit an offer for supplies and services. The successful offerer is selected on the basis of criteria established by the agency's contracting office and the program offices for which the work is to be performed.

Competition Advocate: Senior official appointed to promote full and open competition in the acquisition of supplies and services by the agency.

Comprehensive Procurement Guidelines (CPG):   Designates items that must contain recycled content when purchased by federal, state, and local agencies, or by contractors using appropriated federal funds, when these agencies spend more than $10,000 a year on any of the designated items. For example, if a state agency spends more than $10,000 a year on copy paper and part of that money is from appropriated federal funds, then that state agency must follow the expanded polystyrene (EPS) guidelines and buy 30 percent postconsumer recycled paper (Section 6002 of the Resource Conservation and Recovery Act [RCRA] and Presidential Executive Order 13101).

Consideration: Something of value given or done as recompense that is exchanged by two parties; that which binds a contract.

Contract: A mutually binding legal relationship obligating the contractor to furnish the supplies or services and the agency to pay for them. It includes all types of commitments that obligate agencies to an expenditure of funds that, except as otherwise authorized, are in writing. In addition to bilateral instruments, contracts include (but are not limited to) awards and notices of awards; job orders or task letters issued under basic ordering agreements; letter contracts; orders, such as purchase orders, under which the contract becomes effective by written acceptance or performance; and bilateral contract modifications. Contracts do not include grants and cooperative agreements covered by 31 United States Code (USC) 6301.

Contract Action: An action resulting in a contract, a modification to a contract, or a delivery order placed against an indefinite-delivery, indefinite-quantity (IDIQ) contract.

Contract Administration: All the activities associated with the oversight of the contractor's performance of a contract, from awards to closeout.

Contract Award: Occurs when the contracting officer (CO) has signed and distributed the contract to, or notified, the contractor.

Contract Quality Requirements: The technical requirements in the contract relating to the quality of the supply or service, those contract clauses prescribing inspection, and other quality controls that are binding to the contractor to assure that the supply or service conforms to the contractual requirements.

Contract Requirements: In addition to specified performance requirements, contract requirements include those defined in the statement of work; specifications, standards, and related documents; management systems; and contract terms and conditions.

Contracting: Purchasing, renting, leasing, or otherwise obtaining supplies or services from nonfederal sources. Contracting includes the description of supplies and services required, the selection and solicitation of sources, the preparation and award of contracts, and all phases of contract administration. It does not include grants or cooperative agreements.

Contracting Office: The office authorized by an agency's senior procurement executive that awards or executes a contract for supplies or services.

Contracting Officer (CO): A person with the authority to enter into, administer, and/or terminate contracts and make related determinations and findings.

Contracting Officer's Representative (COR) or Contracting Officer's Technical Representative (COTR): Individuals identified by program offices who are designated and authorized by the contracting officer (CO) to perform contract administration functions on his or her behalf. The functions of CORs/COTRs are limited to those specifically designated in writing by the CO.

Contractor: An entity in private industry that enters into contracts with an agency to provide supplies or services.

Contractor Team Arrangement: An arrangement in which (1) two or more companies form a partnership or joint venture to act as a potential prime contractor or (2) an agreement by a potential prime contractor is made with one or more other companies to have them act as its subcontractors under a specified government contract or acquisition program. Also called a *teaming agreement*.

Cooperative Agreement: An assistance instrument used when substantial involvement is anticipated between the federal government and the state or local government or other recipient during performance of the contemplated activity.

Cooperative Purchasing: The combining of requirements of two or more governmental units to obtain the benefits of volume purchases and/or reduction in administrative expenses.

Cost Analysis: The review and evaluation of the separate cost elements and proposed profit of a contractor's cost or pricing data. Cost analysis always includes price analysis.

Cost or Pricing Data: Factual and verifiable data that includes (1) direct costs, (2) indirect costs, (3) profit or fee, (4) vendor quotations, (5) information on changes in production methods and in production or purchasing volume, and (6) information on management decisions that could have a significant bearing on costs.

Cost Reimbursement Contracts: Contracts based on payment by an agency to a contractor of allowable, reasonable, and allocable costs incurred in the contract performance to the extent prescribed in the contract. These contracts may not require completion of the contract work but rather the best efforts of the contractor. The types of cost reimbursement contracts include (1) cost, (2) cost sharing, (3) cost-plus-fixed fee (CPFF), (4) cost-plus–incentive fee (CPIF), and (5) cost-plus–award fee (CPAF) contracts.

Cradle-to-Grave: The total concept of a procurement, from inception through development, procurement, performance, and final disposition.

Current Year: The fiscal year in progress. Also called *execution year.*

Dealer: A business that maintains a store, warehouse, or other establishment in which a line or lines of products are kept in inventory and are sold to the public on a wholesale or retail basis. Also called *jobber* or *distributor.*

Debarment: The disqualification of a person to receive invitations for bids or requests for proposals or the award of a contract by a government body for a specified time commensurate with the seriousness of the offense, the failure, or the inadequacy of performance.

Default: Failure by a party to a contract to comply with contractual requirements.

Defective Pricing: Inaccurate cost/pricing data, to include delivery orders placed against Federal Supply Schedules (FSS), certified by a contractor to be accurate, current, and complete.

Defense Acquisition Regulatory Council (DARC): A group composed of representatives from each military department, the Defense Logistics Agency, and the National Aeronautics and Space Administration (NASA) that is in charge of the Federal Acquisition Regulations (FAR) on a joint basis with the Civilian Agency Acquisition Council (CAAC).

Defense Contractor: Any person who enters into a contract with the United States for the production of material or for the performance of services for the national defense.

Deliverable: A report or product that must be delivered to the government by the contractor to satisfy contractual requirements.

Delivery: The formal handing over of property; the transfer of possession, such as by carrier to purchaser.

Demurrage: The detention of a ship, railroad car, or truck beyond a specified time for loading/unloading; the payment required and made for the delay.

Dependability: A measure of the degree to which an item is operable and capable of performing its required function at any time during the life of the contract.

Design Specification: A specification setting forth the required characteristics to be considered for award of a contract, including sufficient detail to show how the product is to be manufactured.

Destination: The place to which a shipment is consigned.

Determining the Extent of Competition: The solicitation of three sources meets the requirement for maximum practicable competition for orders of $25,000 or less. However, three is just a guideline. A list of sources should be maintained and continuously updated. The list should contain the status of each source (i.e., small business, veteran-owned small business, small disadvantaged business, woman-owned small business) to ensure that small businesses are afforded opportunities to compete for simplified acquisitions. When using simplified acquisitions, maximum practical competition may be obtained without soliciting quotations or offers from sources outside the local trade area.

Direct Cite: Money does not go through the information technology (IT) fund. It is paid by the agency through the Defense Finance and Accounting Service (DFAS). The vendor must go to the DFAS to settle their account; it does not go through the General Services Administration (GSA). This money expires at the end of the fiscal year and is issued on a 1155 instead of GSA Form 300. Note: Not recommended to use unless IT fund is low.

Direct Cost: Any cost specifically identified as a final cost objective for a particular contract action. Includes cost factors such as direct labor and materials.

Direct Labor: Labor required to complete a product or service; includes fabrication, assembly, inspection, and test for constructing an end product. Also, the labor expended by contractor personnel in performing contractual requirements.

Direct Materials: Includes raw materials, purchased parts, and subcontracted items required to manufacture and assemble completed products. A *direct material cost* is the cost of material used in making a product.

Disbursements: In budgetary usage, gross disbursements represent the amount of checks, cash, or other payments issued, less refunds received.

Distrubutor: See **Dealer**.

Document Type: Used by the Minnesota Accounting and Procurement System (MAPS) to differentiate among different functions for a requisition, solicitation, contract, or order. The document type is a field to be entered on those screens that are for requisition solicitation, contract, or order.

Drop Shipment: Merchandise that is shipped by a manufacturer directly to a customer in response to the seller who collects orders but does not maintain an inventory.

Economically Disadvantaged-Area Business: Small business eligible for certification as socially disadvantaged business or economically disadvantaged-area business; a small business entity with its principal place of business in Minnesota organized for profit, including an individual, partnership, corporation, joint venture, association, or cooperative that is 51 percent owned and is operationally controlled on a day-to-day basis by citizens of the United States. The areas of economic disadvantage are determined by the U.S. Department of Labor.

Effective Competition: A market condition that exists when two or more contractors, acting independently, actively compete for an agency's business in a manner that ensures that the agency will be offered the lowest price or best technical design to meet its minimum needs.

Electronic Data Interchange: Transmission of information between computers using highly standardized electronic versions of common business documents.

Emergency Acquisition: A threat to public health, welfare, or safety that threatens the functioning of government, the protection of property, or the health or safety of people.

Emerging Small Business: A small business concern whose size is no greater than 50 percent of the numerical size standard applicable to the Standard Industrial Classification (SIC) code assigned to a contracting opportunity.

Energy Star: A federal standard applied to office equipment for the purpose of rating the energy efficiency of the equipment. Energy Star computers, monitors, and printers save energy by powering down and going to sleep when not in use, resulting in a reduction in electrical bills and pollution levels.

Environmentally Preferable Product (EPP): A product or service that has a lesser or reduced impact on human health and the environment when compared with competing products or services that serve the same purpose. Such products or services may include, but are not limited to, those that contain recycled content, minimize waste, conserve energy or water, and reduce the amount of toxics either disposed of or consumed.

Equal or Approved Equal: A term used to indicate that an item may be substituted for a required item if it is equal in quality, performance, and other characteristics.

Equity: An accounting term used to describe the net investment of owners or stockholders in a business. Under the accounting equation, equity also represents the result of assets, less liabilities.

Escalation Clause: A contract provision that permits the adjustment of contract prices by an amount or percentage if certain specified contingencies occur, such as changes in the vendor's raw material or labor costs.

Evaluation Criteria: Standards that are used to evaluate an offerer's technical and operational effectiveness.

Evaluation of Responses: The examination of responses after opening to determine the vendor's responsibility, responsiveness to requirements, and other characteristics of the solicitation relating to the award.

Expenditure: A charge against available funds, evidenced by a voucher or claim. Expenditure represents the actual payment of funds.

Facilities Contract: Provides for the procurement, construction, and installation of facilities or the use, maintenance, management, accountability, or disposition of facilities.

Fair and Reasonable Price: A price that is fair to both parties, considering the agreed-upon conditions, promised quality, and timeliness of contract performance; subject to statutory and regulatory limitations.

Federal Acquisition Regulations (FAR): The body of regulations that is the primary source of authority governing the government procurement process. The FAR, which is published as Chapter 1 of Title 48 of the Code of Federal Regulations, is prepared, issued, and maintained under the joint auspices of the secretary of defense, the administrator of the General Services Administration (GSA), and the administrator of the National Aeronautics and Space Administration (NASA). Actual responsibility for maintenance and revision of the FAR is vested jointly in the Defense Acquisition Regulatory Council (DARC) and the Civilian Agency Acquisition Council (CAAC).

Federal Information Processing (FIP): A machine or group of interconnected machines consisting of input, storage, computing, control, and output services. These services function by using electronic circuitry in the main computing element to perform logical operations automatically through internally stored or externally controlled programmed instruction. The term *FIP resources* refers to all computer-related resources, including computer hardware, firmware, software, personnel, documentation, supplies, and support services.

Federal Supply Schedule (FSS) Program: A simplified process for procuring commonly used supplies or services by placing delivery orders against FSS contracts that have been awarded by the General Services Administration (GSA) for use by all agencies.

Firmware: Software that is built into integrated circuits in a permanent or semipermanent form. Firmware lies midway between hardware and software in terms of performance and flexibility.

Fiscal Year: The 12 months between one annual settlement of financial accounts and the next; a term used for budgeting and so forth. The fiscal year for the U.S. government is October 1 to September 30.

Fixed Assets: State property that is in one of four categories:
1. All nonexpendable property having a normal life expectancy of more than two years and a value of $2,000 or more.
2. All semiexpendable property established by the owning agency's policy as fixed assets; any item having a normal life expectancy of more than two years and a value of less than $2,000.
3. All firearms, regardless of their value.
4. All sensitive items, as established by the agency's policy.

Fixed Price Contract: A type of contract that provides for a firm price or, under appropriate circumstances, for an adjustable price for the supplies or services being procured.

Formal Solicitation: A solicitation that requires a sealed response.

Fraud: Acts of fraud or corruption or attempts to defraud an agency or to corrupt its agents; acts that constitute a cause for debarment or suspension under the Federal Acquisition Regulations (FAR) 9.4062(a) and 9.407-2(a); and acts that violate the False Claims Act, 31 U.S. Code (USC), Sections 3729 to 3731, or the Anti-Kickback Act, 41 USC, Sections 51 and 54.

FTE: Full-time employee.

Full and Open Competition: A term indicating that all responsible sources are permitted to compete.

Full and Open Competition After Exclusion of Sources: A term indicating that all responsible sources that meet certain criteria, such as business size or location in a labor surplus area, are permitted to compete. These competitions are specifically authorized by the Competition in Contracting Act (CICA).

General Services Administration (GSA): The agency responsible for the Federal Supply Schedules (FSS) and for buying and leasing office space on behalf of the executive branch.

Goods: All types of personal property, including commodities, materials, supplies, and equipment.

Government Property: Equipment and facilities furnished by the government to a contractor or recipient or acquired by a contractor or recipient at the government's expense for use during the performance of a contract or assistance agreement.

Grant: An assistance instrument used when little federal government involvement is anticipated in the performance by the recipient.

Grants Officer: A contracting officer (CO) who contractually obligates the government by awarding grants.

Hazardous Waste: Any waste (solid, liquid, or gas) that, because of its quantity, concentration, or chemical, physical, or infectious characteristics, poses a substantial present or potential hazard to human health or the environment when improperly treated, stored, transported, or disposed of.

Improper Influence: An influence that induces or tends to induce a federal employee to consider awarding a federal contract or purchase on any basis other than its merit.

Incremental Funding: Used if the total task order is awarded and the dollar amount of the work is more than the client has available as the desired start time. Pricing for the project is totaled and assigned on the contract, but the pricing is charged incrementally as it becomes available. The overall scope of work and pricing does not change from the original proposal. The incremental funds are added by modifications, but the modifications are not supposed to add onto the period of performance or to add money onto the full amount of the contract.

Independent Verifications and Validation Contract (IVV or IV&V):   Contracts through which testing and validation of developed software is accomplished by someone other than the developer.

Informal Solicitation: A solicitation that does not require a sealed response.

Information Technology (IT) Fund: A fund that is managed by the government from which agencies draw to pay their costs. It is "no year money," meaning that it does not expire at the end of the fiscal year. It must be used to buy IT services and supplies.

Insurance: A contract between an insurance company and a person or group that provides for payment in case of covered loss, accident, or death.

Interested Party: A prime contractor or an actual or perspective offerer whose direct economic interest would be affected by the award of a contract or by the failure to award a contract.

Intermediary Organizations: Organizations that play a fundamental role in encouraging, promoting, and facilitating business-to-business (B2B) linkages and mentor-protégé partnerships. These can include both nonprofit and for-profit organizations: chambers of commerce; trade associations; local, civic, and community groups; state and local governments; academic institutions; and private corporations.

Invoice: A list of goods or services sent to a purchaser that shows information including prices, quantities, and shipping charges for payment.

Jobber: See **Dealer**.

Joint Venture: The temporary association of two or more businesses to secure and fulfill a procurement bid award. In the Small Business Administration (SBA) mentor-protégé program, this is an agreement between a certified 8(a) firm and a mentor firm to perform a specific federal contract.

Justification and Analysis (J&A):   Required for any sole source open market procurement *over $100,000* that exceeds the simplified acquisition threshold. This J&A must have a statement from the client as to why the procurement is required to be sole source, and a justification from the General Services Administration (GSA) must accompany this in the official file.

For procurements *over $500,000*, if a client requests a sole source or a particular brand name, they must indicate why and document it. An internal document is prepared and signed by the contract specialist, contracting officer (CO), contracts program director, and competition advocate. A routing slip, an internal document that circulates through the GSA for signatures, is used as a cover sheet for this document, and the attachments are as follows (copies of):

- J&A

- Quote

- Funding document (Military Interagency Purchase Request [MIPR])

Kickback: Any money, fee, commission, credit, gift, gratuity, thing of value, or compensation of any kind that is provided, directly or indirectly, to agency procurement or program officials by any prime contractor employee, subcontractor, or subcontractor employee for the purpose of improperly obtaining or receiving favorable treatment in connection with obtaining a contract.

Labor Surplus Area: A civil jurisdiction designated by the U.S. Department of Labor, usually updated annually in late fall; used as one of the criteria for designating economically disadvantaged vendors.

Lead Time: The time that it would take a supplier to deliver goods after receipt of order.

Lease: A contract conveying from one entity to another the use of real or personal property for a designated period of time in return for payment or other consideration.

Less-Than-Truckload (LTL): A quantity of freight less than the amount necessary to constitute a truckload.

Lessee: One to whom a lease is granted.

Lessor: One who grants a lease.

Life-Cycle Costing: A procurement evaluation technique that determines the total cost of acquisition, operation, maintenance, and disposal of the items acquired; the lowest ownership cost during the time the item is in use.

Line Item: An item of supply or service specified in a solicitation for which the vendor must specify a separate price.

Liquidated Damages: A specific sum of money agreed to as part of a contract to be paid by one party to the other in the event of a breach of contract in lieu of actual damages, unless otherwise provided by law.

List Price: The price of an article published in a catalog, advertisement, or printed list from which discounts, if any, may be subtracted.

Lowest Responsible Vendor: The vendor with the lowest price whose past performance, reputation, and financial capability is deemed acceptable.

Mandatory: Required by the order stipulated (e.g., a specification or specific description that may not be waived).

Manufacturer: A business that makes or processes raw materials into a finished product.

Market: The aggregate forces (including economics) at work in trade and commerce in a specific service or commodity; to sell, analyze, advertise, package, and so on.

Market Research: Also known as *market survey;* involves obtaining information specific to the item being purchased. The extent of market research will vary, depending on such factors as urgency, estimated dollar value, complexity of the requirement, and past experience. Some techniques for conducting market research may include any or all of the following:

- Contracting experts regarding capabilities to meet requirements.

- Reviewing the results of recent market research undertaken to meet similar or identical requirements.

- Publishing formal requests for information in appropriate technical and scientific journals.

- Querying government databases that provide information relevant to agency acquisitions.

- Participating in interactive online communication among the industry, acquisition personnel, and customers.

- Obtaining source lists of similar items from other contracting activities or agencies, trade associations, or other sources.

Marketing Partner Identification Number (MPIN):   A personal code that allows you to access other government applications such as the Past Performance Information Retrieval System (PPIRS) and the Online Representations and Certifications Application (ORCA). The MPIN acts as your password in these other systems, and you should guard it as such. It is a mandatory data element created by the Central Contractor Registration (CCR) registrant and must have nine characters: at least one letter (upper- or lower-case) and one number. No spaces or special characters are permitted.

Material Variance / Material Deviation: A variance or deviation in a response from specifications of conditions that allows a responder a substantial advantage or benefit not enjoyed by all other responders or that gives the state something significantly different from what it requested in the solicitation document.

Materials Management: Embraces all functions of acquisition, standards, quality control, and surplus property management.

Mentor: A business, usually large, or other organization that has created a specialized program to advance strategic relationships with small businesses.

Military Interagency Purchase Request (MIPR): A funding-source document accessed through the Information Technology Solutions Shop (ITSS) for all branches of the military. Be sure to make certain the amount on the MIPR is more than or the same as the contracted amount.

Model Procurement Code (MPC): A publication approved by the American Bar Association that sets forth procurement statutory principles and policy guidelines for managing and controlling the procurement of supplies, services, and construction for public purposes; administrative and judicial remedies for the resolution of controversies relating to public contracts; and a set of ethical standards governing public and private participants in the procurement process.

Modification: Authorized changes to a contract after contract award.

The following lists possible types of modifications:

- *Administrative change:* A unilateral contract change that does not affect the contractual rights of the parties (e.g., a change in the paying office).

- *Change order:* A written order, signed by the contracting officer (CO), directing the contractor to make a change authorized by the "changes clause." A change order is issued without the consent of the contractor.

- *Supplemental agreement:* A contract modification that is accomplished by the mutual action of both parties.

- *Bilateral modification:* A contract modification that is signed by the contractor and the CO; used to make negotiated adjustments resulting from the issuance of a change order, for definitive letter contracts, or to reflect other agreements of the parties modifying the terms of contracts.

- *Unilateral modification:* A contract modification that is signed only by the CO; used to make administrative changes, to issue change orders, or to make changes authorized by something other than a "changes clause."

Multiple Award: Contracts awarded to more than one supplier for comparable supplies and services. Awards are made for the same generic types of items at various prices.

National Association of Purchasing Management (NAPM): A nonprofit educational and technical organization of purchasing and materials management personnel and buying agencies from the public and private sectors.

National Association of State Purchasing Officials (NASPO): An organization of state procurement representatives for the purpose of promoting efficient and effective public purchasing policies and procedures at the state level. The NASPO is an affiliate of the Control of State Governments (CSG).

National Institute of Governmental Purchasing (NIGP): A nonprofit, educational, and technical-assistance corporation of public purchasing agencies and activities at the federal, state, and local levels of government.

Negotiation: Contracting through the use of either competitive or other-than-competitive proposals and discussions. Any contract awarded without using sealed bidding procedures is a negotiated contract. Requests for proposals (RFPs) are sometimes used as a starting point for negotiations to establish a contract. Generally, RFPs include more than just price considerations. This method is especially applicable when dealing with a single source manufacturer.

Net Price: Price after all discounts, rebates, and so on, have been allowed.

No Bid: A response to a solicitation for bids stating that the respondent does not wish to submit an offer. It usually operates as a procedure consideration to prevent suspension from the vendors list for failure to submit a response.

North American Industry Classification System (NAICS) Code: Classification of business established by type of activity for the purpose of facilitating the collection, tabulation, presentation, and analysis of data collected by various agencies of the U.S. government, state agencies, trade associations, and private research organizations for promoting uniformity and comparability in the presentation of statistical data relating to those establishments and their fields of endeavor; formerly known as the Standard Industrial Classification (SIC) code.

Offer: A response to a solicitation that, if accepted, binds the offerer to fulfill the resulting contract. Responses to invitations for bids (IFB) are called *bids* or *sealed bids;* responses to requests for proposals (RFP) are referred to as *offers* or *proposals;* and responses to requests for quotations (RFQ) are designated as *quotes*.

Office of Small and Disadvantaged Business Utilization (OSDBU): Section 15(K) of the Small Business Act (Public Law 95-507; October 24, 1978) establishes an OSDBU in each federal agency having procurement powers. Furthermore, it directs the management of each such office be vested in an officer or employee of such an agency, known as the director of small and disadvantaged business utilization, who should, among other things:

- Be appointed by the head of such agency.
- Be responsible only to, and report directly to, the head of such agency or to his or her deputy.
- Be responsible for the implementation and execution of the functions and duties under Sections 8 and 15 of the Small Business Act.
- Have supervisory authority over personnel of such agency to the extent that the functions and duties of such personnel relate to functions and duties included under Sections 8 and 15 of the act.
- Assign a small business technical advisor to each office to which the administration has assigned a procurement center representative, a person (1) who should be a full-time employee of the procuring activity and should be well qualified, technically trained, and familiar with the supplies or services purchased at the activity; and (2) whose principal duty is to assist the administration procurement center representative in his or her duties and functions relating to Sections 8 and 15 of the Small Business Act.
- Cooperate, and consult on a regular basis, with the administration with respect to carrying out the functions and duties listed in Sections 8 and 15 of the Small Business Act.

One–Stop Capital Shops (OSCSs): The Small Business Administration's (SBA) contribution to the Empowerment Zones/Enterprise Communities Program, an interagency initiative that provides resources to economically distressed communities. The shops provide a full range of SBA lending and technical-assistance programs.

Open Market Requisition (OMR):   The requisition document type used in the Minnesota Accounting and Procurement System (MAPS) to request the purchase of a noncontract item when the requested item's estimated cost exceeds the authority for purchase level of the buyer. An OMR conveys the request for purchase to the person with the authority to purchase. The resulting order type is most often the purchase order requisition (POR).

Option: A clause contained in a contract that gives an agency the unilateral right to extend the term of the contract or obtain additional quantities of products or services at the prices contained in the contract for that option period or additional quantity of products or services.

Orders: Work orders against an existing contract for hardware/software.

Organizational Conflict of Interest: Activities or relationships with other persons that interfere with the ability of a contractor or contractor employee to render impartial assistance or advice to an agency.

OSHA: Occupational Safety and Health Administration; created by the OSHA Act.

Other Direct Costs (ODCs):   The costs of facilities, supplies, and services provided by the contractor in support of task order performance that would normally be provided by the government. The Compensation System Review (CSR) shall determine that the proposed costs are necessary, and the authorized contracting officer (ACO) shall determine that the prices are fair and reasonable.

Packing List: A document that itemizes in detail the contents of a particular package or shipment.

Partial Payment: The payment authorized in a contract upon delivery of one or more units called for under the contract or upon completion of one or more distinct items of service called for thereunder.

Parties Excluded from Procurement Programs: Contractors included on the "Consolidated List of Debarred,

Suspended, and Ineligible Contractors." This list is compiled, maintained, and distributed by the General Services Administration (GSA).

Partnering: A mutually beneficial business-to-business (B2B) relationship based on trust and commitment and that enhances the capabilities of both parties.

Per Diem: By the day.

Performance Bond: A contract of guarantee that is executed subsequent to award by a successful vendor to protect the buyer from loss due to the vendor's inability to complete the contract as agreed.

Performance Specification: A specification setting forth performance requirements determined necessary for the item involved to perform and last as required.

Plant-Matter-Based or Bio-Based Product: A product derived from renewable resources, including fiber crops, such as kenaf; chemical extracts from oilseeds, nuts, fruits, and vegetables (such as corn and soybeans); agricultural residues, such as wheat straw and corn stover; and wood wastes generated from processing and manufacturing operations. These products stand in contrast to those made from fossil fuels (such as petroleum) and other less renewable resources (such as virgin timber).

Point of Origin: The location where a shipment is received by a transportation line from the shipper; also known as the *shipping point*.

Political Subdivision: A subdivision of a state that has been delegated certain functions of local government; can include counties, cities, towns, villages, hamlets, boroughs, and parishes.

Postconsumer Material: A finished material that would normally be disposed of as a solid waste after its life cycle as a consumer item is completed; does not include manufacturing or converting wastes. This refers to material collected for recycling from office buildings, homes, retail stores, and so on.

PPIRS: Past Performance Information Retrieval System.

Preaward Survey: An evaluation by a contracting activity of a prospective contractor's capability to perform a proposed contract. Site visits to contractor facilities are often conducted to determine qualifications and eligibility to receive awards.

Preconsumer Material: Material or by-products generated after the manufacture of a product but before the product reaches the consumer, such as damaged or obsolete products. Preconsumer material does not include mill and manufacturing trim, scrap, or broken material that is generated at a manufacturing site and commonly reused on-site in the same or another manufacturing process.

Preference: An advantage in consideration for award of a contract granted to a vendor by reason of the vendor's residence, business location, or business classifications (e.g., minority owned, small business, and so on).

Prepaid: A term denoting that transportation charges have been or are to be paid at the point of shipment.

Prequalification of Vendors: The screening of potential vendors in which such factors as financial capability, reputation, and management are considered when developing a list of qualified vendors. See **Vendors List** and **Qualified Vendor**.

Price: The amount of money that will purchase a definite weight or other measure of a commodity.

Price Agreement: A contractual agreement in which a purchaser contracts with a vendor to provide the purchaser's requirements at a predetermined price; usually involves a minimum number of units—orders placed directly with the vendor by the purchaser—and limited duration of the contract. See **Blanket Order** and **Requirements Contract**.

Price Analysis: The process of examining and evaluating a proposed price by comparing it with other offered prices or prices previously paid for similar goods or services.

Price Fixing: An agreement among competing vendors to sell at the same price.

Price Negotiation Memorandum: A document that is used if the General Services Administration (GSA) enters negotiations and indicates the prices are fair and reasonable; done with all 8(a)s over $100,000.

Prime Contract: A contract awarded directly by the federal government.

Prime Contractor: A corporation, partnership, business association, trust, joint-stock company, educational institution, or other nonprofit organization or individual who has entered into a prime contract with an agency.

Procurement: The combined functions of purchasing, inventory control, traffic and transportation, receiving, inspection, storekeeping, and salvage and disposal operations.

Procurement Activity: The organization within an agency authorized to enter into contractual relationships.

Procurement Automated Source System (PASS): A database managed by the Small Business Administration (SBA) that contains information on over 230,000 small businesses. The PASS database must be queried and reviewed by agency personnel to locate potential contractors. Not all small businesses are included in the PASS database, but it does represent a good sampling of the availability of business in a particular industry. One of the primary reasons for using the PASS search is that if any sources are found, the results are included in the "Justification for Other than Full and Open Competition" (JOFOC).

Procurement Center Reprsentative (PCR): Small Business Administration (SBA) representatives assigned to federal agencies to assist in conducting their small business programs by recommending sources and the use of appropriate set-asides. These PCRs have the authority to challenge a contracting officer's (CO) decision not to conduct a particular procurement as a set-aside; they also review and make recommendations on proposed subcontracting plans.

Procurement List: A list of supplies and services that the Committee for Purchase from People Who Are Blind or Severely Disabled has determined to be available for mandatory purchase by federal agencies.

Procurement Official: Any civilian or military official or employee of an agency who has participated personally and substantially in any of the following activities for a particular procurement:

1. Drafting a specification or a statement of work for that procurement.
2. Reviewing or approving a specification or statement of work developed for that procurement.
3. Preparing or developing procurement or purchase requests for that procurement.
4. Preparing or issuing a solicitation for that procurement.
5. Evaluating bids or proposals for that procurement.
6. Selecting sources for that procurement.
7. Negotiating to establish the price or terms and conditions of a particular contract or contract modification.
8. Reviewing and approving the award of a contract or contract modification (Federal Acquisition Regulation [FAR], 3.104-4,[h][1]).

Procurement Plan: Completed for 8(a) businesses and provides an outline of actions for the contract; an internal document on which the contract specialist and contracting officer (CO) sign off.

Proprietary: The only items that can perform a function and satisfy a need. This should not be confused with "single source." An item can be proprietary and yet available from more than one source. For example, if you need a camera lens for a Nikon camera, the only lens that will fit is a Nikon lens; thus, this lens is proprietary. However, the Nikon lens is available from more than one source; thus, it is not single source.

Protégé: A firm in a developmental stage that aspires to increase its capabilities through a mutually beneficial business-to-business (B2B) relationship.

Protest: Written objection by an interested party to a procurement action conducted by an agency.

Public Purchasing: The process of obtaining goods and services for public purpose by following procedures implemented to protect public funds from being expended extravagantly or capriciously.

Purchase Manual: A document that stipulates rules and prescribes procedures for purchasing with suppliers and other departments.

Purchase Order: An offer made by an agency to buy certain supplies or nonpersonal services from commercial sources and based on specified terms and conditions. The aggregate amount shall not exceed the small purchase limit—currently $100,000.

Purchase Request (PR):   A document that is used to initiate a procurement action. Whether referred to as a PR, a *requisition*, or a *procurement directive*, it provides the necessary authorization to proceed with a procurement.

Qualified Film Producers List (QFPL):   A list of producers qualified to make government film productions. The Department of Defense (DoD) Federal Audiovisual Contract Management Office (FACMO) maintains this list.

Qualified Products List (QPL):   A list of products that, because of the length of time required for test and evaluation, are tested in advance of procurement to determine which suppliers comply with the specification requirements; also referred to as an *approved brands list*.

Qualified Vendor: A vendor that is determined by a buying organization to meet minimum set standards of business competence, reputation, financial ability, and product quality for placement on the vendors list; also known as a *responsible vendor*.

Qualified Video Producers List (QVPL):   A list of producers qualified to make government video productions. The Department of Defense (DoD) Federal Audiovisual Contract Management Office (FACMO) maintains this list.

Quality: The composite of material attributes, including performance features and characteristics, of a product or service to satisfy a given need.

Quantity: Amount or number.

Quantity Discount: A reduction in the unit price offered for large volume contracts.

Ratification: The process used by an agency's contracting officers (CO) to approve and legitimize an otherwise proper contract made by an individual without contracting authority.

Recycled Content: The portion of a product that is made from materials directed from the waste stream; usually stated as a percentage by weight.

Recycled Product: A product that contains the highest amount of postconsumer material practicable, or, when postconsumer material is impracticable for a specific type of product, a product that contains substantial amounts of preconsumer material.

Remanufactured Product: Any product diverted from the supply of discarded materials by refurbishing and marketing the product without making substantial changes to its original form.

Request for Bid (RFB):   A solicitation in which the terms, conditions, and specifications are described and responses are not subject to negotiation.

Request for Proposal (RFP):   A solicitation in which it is not advantageous to set forth all the actual detailed requirements at the time of solicitation and responses are subject to negotiation. Price must be a factor in the award but not the sole factor.

Request for Proposal (RFP) or Request for Bid (RFB) Conference: A meeting arranged by a procurement office to help potential bidders understand the requirements of an RFP or an RFB.

Requirements: Materials, personnel, or services needed for a specific period of time.

Requirements Contract: A form of contract that is used when the total long-term quantity required cannot be definitely fixed but can be stated as an estimate or within maximum and minimum limits with deliveries on demand.

Requisition: An internal document that a functional department (stores, maintenance, production, and so on) sends to the purchasing department that contains details of materials to meet its needs, to replenish stocks, or to obtain materials for specific jobs or contracts.

Resident Vendor: A person, firm, or corporation authorized to conduct business in a particular state on the date a solicitation for a contract is first advertised or announced. It includes a foreign corporation duly authorized to engage in business in that state.

Responder: One who submits a response to a solicitation.

Response: The offer received from a vendor in response to a solicitation. A response includes submissions commonly referred to as *offers*, *bids*, *quotes*, or *proposals*.

Responsible Bidder: A bidder whose reputation, past performance, and business and financial capabilities are such that the bidder would be judged by an appropriate authority as capable of satisfying an organization's needs for a specific contract.

Responsive Bidder: A bidder whose bid does not vary from the specifications and terms set out in the invitation for bids.

Restrictive Specifications: Specifications that unnecessarily limit competition by eliminating items capable of satisfactorily meeting actual needs. See **Performance Specification**.

Reused Product: Any product designed to be used many times for the same or a different purpose without additional processing other than specific requirements, such as cleaning, painting, or minor repairs.

Sealed Bid: A method determined by the commissioner to prevent the contents from being revealed or known before the deadline for submission of responses.

Senior Procurement Executive: An executive for an agency who is appointed by the agency head pursuant to Section 16(3) of the Office of Federal Procurement Policy

(OFPP) Act (41 U.S. Code [USC] 414[3]) and who is responsible for managing the agency's procurement activities.

Sensitive Compartmented Information Facility (SCIF): A facility that provides formal access controls.

Service Corps of Retired Executives (SCORE): A 12,400-member volunteer association sponsored by the Small Business Administration (SBA) that matches volunteer business management counselors with present prospective small business owners in need of expert advice.

Services: Unless otherwise indicated, both professional or technical services and services performed under a service contract.

SES: Senior Executive Service, or a member of the SES.

Settlement Agreement: A written agreement, in the form of a modification to a contract, settling all or a severable portion of a settlement proposal resulting from the termination of a contract for the convenience of the agency.

Single Source: An acquisition where, after a search, only one supplier is determined to be reasonably available for the required product, service, or construction item.

SLED: An acronym that stands for the market segment of state and local government and education.

Small Business: A designation for certain statutory purposes referring to a firm, corporation, or establishment that has a small number of employees, low volume of sales, small amount of assets, or limited impact on the market.

Small Business Development Centers (SBDCs): Offer a broad spectrum of business information and guidance as well as assistance in preparing loan applications.

Small Business Innovative Research (SBIR) Contract: A type of contract designed to foster technological innovation by small businesses with 500 or fewer employees. The SBIR contract program provides for a three-phased approach to research and development projects: technological feasibility and concept development; the primary research effort; and the conversion of the technology to a commercial application.

Small Disadvantaged Business Concern: A small business concern that is at least 51 percent owned by one or more individuals who are both socially and economically disadvantaged. This can include a publicly owned business that has at least 51 percent of its stock unconditionally owned by one or more socially and economically disadvantaged individuals and whose management and daily business is controlled by one or more such individuals.

Small Purchase: A term that currently applies to procurements with thresholds of $100,000 or less. The Federal Acquisition Streamlining Act (FASA) has replaced the current term and threshold for *small purchase* with a new term called *simplified acquisition threshold* whose threshold includes procurements of $100,000 or less. There are two purchase categories under the simplified acquisition threshold. Purchases under $3,000 are called *micropurchases*. For these purchases, the small purchase set-aside for small business is dissolved. Small business reservation does apply to values of $3,001 to $100,000. If an agency has interim or full Federal Acquisition Computer Network (FACNET) capability, which is the ability to perform certain functions electronically, the $100,000 threshold on simplified acquisitions applies; otherwise, the threshold is $50,000. The higher threshold for simplified acquisition supports the acquisition streamlining initiative and provides small business contractors with increased set-aside opportunities.

Software: A combination of associated computer instructions and computer data definitions required to enable computer hardware to perform computational or control functions.

Sole Source Procurement: A contract for the purchase of supplies or services that is entered into by an agency after soliciting and negotiating with only one source. Such procurements must be fully justified to indicate the reasons why competition is not possible.

Solicitation: A formal document that elicits proposals for acquisition or financial assistance awards. Solicitation instruments include invitations for bid (IFB), requests for proposals (RFP), and for small purchase actions, requests for quotations (RFQ).

Solutions for Enterprise-Wide Procurement (SEWP) Contracts: National Aeronautics and Space Administration (NASA) contracts that have been precompeted so that no additional competition is required; NASA charges a 0.75 percent access fee. The SEWP is an indefinite-delivery, indefinite-quantity (IDIQ) government-wide acquisition contract (GWAC), now in its fourth iteration.

Source Reduction Product: A product that results in a net reduction in the generation of waste and includes durable, reusable, and remanufactured products; products with no packaging or with reduced packaging.

Source Selection Plan: A document that explains how proposals from offerers will be evaluated. The plan includes the evaluation factors to be used, the relative weight of the factors, and the methodology to be used by evaluators in evaluating proposals.

Specification: A concise statement of a set of requirements to be satisfied by a product, material, or process that indicates whenever appropriate the procedures to determine whether the requirements are satisfied. As far as practicable, it is desirable that the requirements are expressed numerically in terms of appropriate units, together with their limits. A specification may be a standard, a part of a standard, or independent of a standard.

Spot Reductions: A small reduction from one's regular GSA Schedule price for a specific agency; usually a one-time event.

Standard: An item's characteristic or set of characteristics generally accepted by the manufacturers and users of the item as required for all such items.

Standard Industrial Classification (SIC) Code: A code representing a category within the SIC system administered by the statistical policy division of the U.S. Office of Management and Budget. The SIC has been replaced by the

North American Industry Classification System (NAICS) for federal contracting.

Standardization: The process of defining and applying the conditions necessary to ensure that a given range of requirements can normally be met, with minimal variety, in a reproducible and economic manner based on the best current techniques.

Subcontract: A contract between a prime contractor and another source to obtain outside supplies for services that the prime contractor needs to perform the contract requirements. Subcontracts include any agreement, other than an employer-employee relationship, into which a prime contractor enters for the purpose of fulfilling a government contract.

Subcontracting Plan: A written plan, submitted by a prime contractor and approved by a contracting officer (CO), that describes the goals and actions the contractor plans to take to use small and small disadvantaged businesses to the maximum practicable extent in performing the contract.

Surplus Property: Property in excess of the needs of an organization and not required for its foreseeable use. Surplus may be used or new, but it possesses some usefulness for the purpose it was intended or for some other purpose.

Tabulation of Responses: The recording of responses for the purposes of comparison, analysis, and record keeping.

TDY: Temporary duty, on travel.

Technical Direction: The direction or guidance of the scientific, engineering, and other technical aspects of a project, as distinguished from the administrative and business management aspects.

Terms and Conditions: A phrase generally applied to the rules under which all bids must be submitted and the stipulations included in most purchase contracts; often published by the purchasing authorities for the information of all potential vendors.

Title: The instrument or document whereby ownership of property is established.

TORT: A wrongful act, other than a breach of contract, such that the law permits compensation of damages.

Truckload (TL): A quantity of freight to which truckload rates apply or a shipment tendered as a truckload; also a highway truck or trailer loaded to its carrying capacity. See **Less-Than-Truckload (LTL)**.

Unauthorized Commitment: The placing of an order, orally or in writing, for supplies or services by an agency employee who does not have a contracting officer (CO) warrant authorizing them to enter into a contract on behalf of the agency; also includes orders placed by contracting officers that exceed their authorized dollar limit.

Uniform Commercial Code (UCC): A comprehensive modernization of various statutes relating to commercial transactions, including sales, leases, negotiable instruments, bank deposits and collections, funds transfers, letters of credit, bulk sales, documents of title, investment securities, and secured transactions.

Unit Price: The price of a selected unit of a good or service (e.g., pound, labor hours, etc.).

Unsettled Contract Charge: Any pending contract change or contract term for which a modification is required, including a change order that has not been negotiated but has been effected.

Unsolicited Proposal: A written proposal that is submitted to an agency by an outside source offering to perform an agency's work more effectively or efficiently. The unsolicited proposal shall not be in response to a formal or informal request unless it is an agency request constituting a publicized general statement of need.

Unsuccessful Vendor: A vendor whose response is not accepted for reasons such as price, quantity, failure to comply with specifications, and so forth.

Value Analysis: An organized effort directed at analyzing the function of systems, products, specifications, standards, practices, and procedures for the purpose of satisfying the required function at the lowest total cost of effective ownership consistent with the requirements for performance, reliability, quality, and maintainability.

Value Engineering: An organized effort to analyze the functions of systems, equipment, facilities, services, and supplies for the purpose of achieving the essential functions at the lowest life-cycle cost consistent with required performance, reliability, quality, and safety.

Vendor: Someone who sells something; a seller.

Vendors List: A list of the names and addresses of suppliers from whom bids, proposals, and quotations might be expected. The list, maintained by the purchasing office, should include all suppliers who have expressed interest in doing business with the government.

Virgin Product: A product that is made with 100 percent new raw materials and contains no recycled materials.

Volatile Organic Compounds (VOCs):   Compounds that evaporate easily at room temperature and often have a sharp smell. They can come from many products, such as office equipment, adhesives, carpeting, upholstery, paints, solvents, and cleaning products. Some VOCs can cause cancer in certain situations, especially when they are concentrated indoors. They also create ozone, a harmful outdoor air pollutant.

Warranty: The representation, either expressed or implied, that a certain fact regarding the subject matter of a contract is presently true or will be true. This is not to be confused with a *guarantee*, which is a contract or promise by one person to answer for the performance of another person.

Woman-Owned Small Business: Companies that meet the definition of a small business and are at least 51 percent owned by a woman or women who are U.S. citizens and who also control and operate the business. The preferred terminology for these businesses is *women business enterprises* (WBEs).

APPENDIX 2

Resources

Judy Bradt of Summit Insight (www.SummitInsight.com) assisted in compiling this list. The full descriptions of these publications, associations, and other pertinent Web sites will be available at www.GovernmentMarketMaster.com.

One additional resource, Federal News Radio, is available at www.FederalNewsRadio.com.

PUBLICATIONS

The following list of publications represents the tip of the iceberg. Most business publications have government readers. If the publication is audited (by the Business Publication Audit or the Audit Bureau of Circulations), read the audit statement to see if your targeted audience is represented.

AFCEA Signal: www.afcea.org/SIGNAL
American City and County: americancityandcounty.com
American School and University: asumag.com
Army Times: www.armytimes.com
Aviation Week: www.aviationweek.com/aw
Better Roads: www.betterroads.com
Defense Systems: defensesystems.com
Defense Technology International: www.defensetechnology
  international.com/about.htm

Emergency Management: www.emergencymgmt.com

Federal Computer Week: www.fcw.com

Federal Times: www.federaltimes.com

FedTech: fedtechmagazine.com

Gov 2.0 Radar: radar.oreilly.com/gov2

Governing: www.governing.com

Government Computer News: www.gcn.com

Government Engineering: www.govengr.com

Government Executive: govexec.com

Government Health IT: govhealthit.com

Government Security News: www.gsnmagazine.com

Government Technology: govtech.com

Government Technology's Public CIO: govtech.com/PCIO

Government Video: www.governmentvideo.com

GovPro (Government Procurement and Government Product News): www.govpro.com

Homeland Security Today: www.hstoday.us

Information Week Government: www.informationweek.com/government

Law Enforcement Product News: www.officer.com

Military & Aerospace Electronics: www.militaryaerospace.com/index.html

NextGov: www.nextgov.com

Procurement: www.nigp.org

Public Manager: thepublicmanager.com

Public Safety IT: www.hendonpub.com/publications/PublicSafetyIT

Washington Technology: washingtontechnology.com

ASSOCIATIONS

American Council on Technology/Industry Advisory Council (ACT/IAC): www.actgov.org

American Small Business Coalition (ASBC): www.theasbc.org

Armed Forces Communications and Electronics Association (AFCEA): www.afcea.org

Association for Federal Information Resources Management (AFFIRM): www.affirm.org

Association of Proposal Management Professionals (APMP): www.apmpnca.org

Association of the U.S. Army: www.ausa.org

Building Owners and Managers Association (BOMA): www.boma.org

Greater Washington Hispanic Chamber of Commerce: www.gwhcc.org

International Facility Managers Association (IFMA): www.ifma.org

National Association of Women Business Owners: www.nawbo.org

National Contract Management Association: www.ncmahq.org

National Defense Industries Association (NDIA): www.ndia.org

National Guard Association of the United States: www.ngaus.org

National Minority Supplier Development Council, Inc.: www.nmsdc.org

Navy League of the United States: www.navyleague.org

Professional Services Council (PSC): www.pscouncil.org

Small and Emerging Contractors Advisory Forum (SECAF): www.secaf.org

Society of American Military Engineers: www.same.org

TechAmerica: www.techamerica.org

Women Impacting Public Policy: www.wipp.org

Women in Defense: wid.ndia.org

Women in Technology: www.womenintechnology.org

Women's Business Centers: www.awbc.biz

APPENDIX 3
Advice from Industry Experts

In the spirit of the idea that all of us are smarter than one of us, in 2009, I asked several of my expert friends and advisors to provide their version of a short list for things CEOs and companies new to the government market. This resulted in an e-book that is available at my blog and now here in a slightly edited format. You have seen my contributions throughout this book, along with several of those that follow and others.

You will see that some of the advice is redundant. It is written this way in the e-book and is intentionally left so here. It is important for the novice to understand that when several seasoned professionals offer the same advice, you might want to pay attention.

Courtney Fairchild, president of Global Services, Inc. (www.GlobalServicesInc.com), a government contract advisory firm, offers the following advice. Global Services provides winning strategies for every stage of marketing to the government, analyzing your opportunities, helping you obtain a GSA Schedule, and building your company's self-sufficiency in federal contracting.

1. *Stick to just one to three agencies to target.*
2. *To decide which agencies to target, do the research to find those that have the greatest need, authority, and budget for your products and services.*

3. *Figure out how the agencies procure.* Which contract vehicles will be needed, given the space you are looking at? Will you need to go through a prime that already has the preferred contract vehicle?

4. *Be realistic about the time it takes to start and grow the government contracting side.* Do you have the resources necessary to dedicate the marketing staff internally and externally, and can you wait for the return for 12 to 16 months?

5. *Find a good organization for networking within the space you have chosen.*

Michael Keating, senior editor of *Government Product News* and *Government Procurement* (www.govpro.com; part of Penton Publishing), is next to offer advice. Michael has been doing research into the government market for two decades.

1. *Research the market.* Use sources such as the GovPro Buyers' Guide (available at www.govpro.com), FedBizOpps, or BidNet to find out if governments are buying your products or services. Even if you see no government purchases or applications, this may simply mean that government buyers and specifiers don't know about what you are selling. Contact the nearest procurement technical assistance center; they can assist you in landing government business. Go here to locate the nearest center: http://www.aptac-us.org/new/Govt_Contracting/find.php. Also, see if any industry trade groups to which your firm belongs have government contracting committees that can assist you in the process of selling to the government.

2. *Determine if your business qualifies as a minority business enterprise (MBE) or for designation as woman owned, small, Native American, or other special business classification.* Maybe there's a set-aside program that can give your firm a leg up on the competition. Also, check out preferences to buy American or buy local that might be applicable.

3. *Register your company with government purchasing offices at all levels of government (federal, state, city, county, township, special district, school district, etc.).* Get on the bidders lists for the products or services your firm is selling, and bid for the business when you get an invitation to bid from governments.

4. *Build a list of government purchasing offices and consuming-agency prospects.* Market your products or services to those installations using all available channels.

5. *Network and spread the word about your products and services and successful applications in government.* Send your government case studies and success stories to *Government Product News* and *Government Procurement* (e-mail: michael .keating@penton.com).

6. *Also, exhibit at conferences for government purchasing officials, such as the National Institute of Governmental Purchasing's annual forum and products exposition.* Go here for details: http://www.nigp.org/events/forum.htm.

Guy Timberlake of the American Small Business Coalition (ASBC; www.theasbc.org) offers his list next. The ASBC is a for-profit business association focused on assisting small companies in doing business in the government sector.

1. *Understand the company resources necessary for standing up/maintaining a government-sector practice.*

2. *Gain an appreciation for the unique differences associated with doing business in this market.*

3. *Manage your expectations.* Know that it will be at least two years before you realize substantial business.

4. *Strategy and focus will be your friend.* Plan your work and work your plan.

5. *Ask lots of questions of prospects, partners, and customers.*

Michael Balsam, vice president of Onvia (www.onvia.com), offers the following advice. Onvia provides current information on upcoming contracts from federal, state, and local government agencies on every type of product and service.

1. *Know your sales cycle*. Government agencies are some of the most reliable clients out there. The rigorous award process provides a lot of transparency, and there's little danger they'll skip town and not pay the bill. However, because of the process involved in government contracting, it can take longer to receive payment for government work—sometimes up to 30 to 45 days after the work is completed. Make sure you factor this longer payment cycle into your budget planning. Can you cover your overhead until the payment comes in?

2. *Build relationships now*. Eighty percent of government contracts are never put up for bid. If a contract is under a certain dollar threshold, the agency is under no obligation to put out a bid or request for proposals (RFP). Government agencies rely on preferred vendors lists and preexisting relationships to fill these contract needs. Start building relationships with decision makers at your target agencies; you never want your bid to be the first time they've heard of your company. Having a solid relationship with government agencies will also help your company get specified on larger-dollar contracts.

3. *Tackle the competition*. The majority of government contractors lose more bids than they win. Research your target agencies' purchasing history to find trends in their buying activities (Do they prefer local contractors or small businesses? Have they awarded the last several projects to the same company?), to make sure it's a project you want to pursue, and research your competitors to position your strengths against their weaknesses. The good news is that government agencies are likely to go with the incumbent on a contract renewal, so once you've won a contract, perform well and you'll drastically increase your chances of winning another project with that agency.

4. *Sweat the small stuff.* A government request for proposals is a seriously dense piece of work. It's about on par with your tax documents, only this involves the government paying you money! However, it's important to read the RFP closely and pay attention to every detail. It's easy to get lost in all the government-speak, but doing so could mean bidding on a project you're ineligible for, having your proposal disqualified on a technicality, or, worst of all, bidding low because of incorrect pricing. You don't want to be awarded a contract you'll lose money on or spend a lot of time and money drafting a proposal for a contract you have no chance of winning.

5. *Stay on top of bid notifications.* Your proposal team will need as much time as possible to draft a killer proposal. The earlier you can find out about an opportunity, the more time your team will have to research, write, and revise the proposal, giving you more of a competitive edge.

The next advice is from Bob Lohfeld, CEO of Lohfeld Consulting (www.LohfeldConsulting.com), the leading bid and proposal, business development, and capture consulting firm. Their clients represent the top tier of contractors in the government market.

1. *Understand your market.* The government market is enormous, and it is made up of many different agencies and buying organizations with different needs and buying preferences. To be effective in selling to the government, you need to understand the market, recognizing which organizations are likely to have an interest in your product or services and which ones are not. Because the market is so large, you must focus and prioritize your pursuit and, as an old fisherman might say, "Fish where there are fish." A good analysis of this market is an essential first step.

2. *Understand why the government might buy your product or service.* You might be surprised to learn that the government

market attracts lots of firms, all trying to sell their product or service. The good thing about the government market is that it is very open about what it plans to buy, assuming you know where to look. The bad thing, from your perspective, is that all your competitors can generally discover the same selling opportunities as you. For that reason, you need a well-thought-out strategy to differentiate your offering from others and a well-defined value proposition that addresses the government's needs. Commercial selling jargon like "increase your profits" will fall on deaf ears with government buyer, whereas "improve service to the citizen" may be just what the government wants to hear. Having your strategy in place and knowing your value proposition before you start selling will keep you from giving up after a few unproductive meetings with government executives.

3. *Know how the government buys.* All government agencies operate under procurement rules defined in the Federal Acquisition Regulations and the many variants of these rules that have been adopted by specific government agencies. These rules seem strange to commercial practitioners but are just part of the learning process you'll go through when you start doing business with Uncle Sam. The government has preferred mechanisms for buying products and services. These range from smaller purchases under GSA Schedule contracts to large multiagency contracts that serve as vehicles to push through billions of dollars in contract awards. You'll need to understand these contract vehicles and be ready to offer one or more as closing mechanisms when your customer wants to buy. Without these, you'll have little chance of selling your wares in the government market.

4. *Be ready to pursue an opportunity.* Going from deal identification to deal closure is called *capture management* in the government market, and successful capture managers can close north of 50 percent of the deals they chase. If you want to

win significant contract awards, you'll be up against some of the best capture managers in the business. There are lots of tricks of the trade that will help you be successful in your pursuits, and a good capture professional can guide along the journey. Capture managers work to discover customer requirements, needs, and preferences; position your firm to win and build customer advocacy in the process; understand your competition and build win strategies and pricing strategies; build and execute teaming and subcontracting agreements; and oversee the development of your proposal. There is a lot to do in closing your deal, and the more experience you have at doing this in the government market, the more likely you are to be successful.

5. *Be ready to write your winning proposal.* Most government procurements of any significant value require you to write a proposal, and proposals are often several hundred pages long and must be written within a few weeks. When the government issues a request for proposal, all serious contenders will snap into high gear, assigning their best and brightest people to the task of writing their proposals. Successful companies have this process well in hand and have ready access to superstar talent needed to write winning proposals. If your company is not an expert at this, then get help. Proposals are major undertakings, and even the largest companies in the government market go outside for talent to manage and write their proposals. This is not an exercise for novices.

6. *Be ready to perform.* In the government market, your past performance will become your key to future success. The government goes to great lengths to track contractor performance and archives this data in various databases that are accessible to all government procurement officials. Because the government places such a high premium on past performance, you must do an outstanding job on your first contract and every contract thereafter. Being risk averse and pursuing only contracts you can perform well will pay

dividends for you in the long run. Be forewarned that for each government procurement you bid, the government will ask you to explain whether your company met the cost, schedule, and technical objectives of your past contracts. The government may cross-reference your answers with past performance databases, and they will call other government agencies to double-check your performance record. Outstanding past performance is indeed a prerequisite for future work.

7. *Be patient and prepared to go the distance.* The government moves at its own pace and will buy when it is ready to buy, not when you are ready to sell. Government executives work their budgets through Congress, often requiring multiple years to get programs approved and funded. They are not moved by your need to book sales at the end of your quarter or because you boss wants to make a big splash with the company's shareholders. For the new practitioner, be ready for a long, hard journey into the competitive world of government contracts. For those who stay the course, the journey can produce significant rewards, but many will run out of resources and patience before their first deal arrives. If you are going to enter this market, be realistic and be patient. Good things will come in time.

Judy Bradt, principal and CEO of Summit Insight (www .SummitInsight.com), offers the following advice. Summit Insight is an advisory firm for small business in the government market.

1. *Get financing.* It takes money to pursue, and then perform, and then stay alive until the government pays you.
2. *Past performance helps you focus.* Look for opportunities most similar to the very best projects you've already done.
3. *FedBizOpps isn't prospecting.* Dramatically increase success and cut costs through research, referrals, and personal introductions.

4. *Use the Offices of Small and Disadvantaged Business Utilization (OSDBUs).* Small business specialists open doors for you if you've done your homework and prepared a kickass capability statement.
5. *Relationships are the whole game.* People do business with people they like and trust, and they help their friends.

The final advice comes from Lisa Dezzutti, president of Market Connections, Inc. (www.MarketConnectionsInc .com), a leading market research firm focusing on the federal government.

1. *Set realistic sales targets, and be willing to make the investment.* Results won't happen overnight. If you're expecting big federal revenues within 6 to 12 months, don't bother getting in the game.
2. *Target the right audience.* You must target the end users of your product or service. Companies that focus their efforts primarily on procurement and contracting personnel fail in this market.
3. *Know the needs and requirements of your targeted end users.* Learn what motivates their behavior. How? Ask them. Use a third-party research firm to survey your target audience.
4. *Act on what you learn.* Adjust your strategies. Fine-tune your messaging and sales approach. Companies that do this achieve double-digit growth rates in the federal market.
5. *Hire someone with federal experience to help your team navigate the world of federal contracting.* Too many companies have gotten in over their heads because they assumed winning and then delivering on a government contract would not be that different than what they have done in the commercial world.

These are just the tip-of-the-iceberg tidbits from some seasoned professionals in this market, people who have witnessed up close what it takes for a company to come in and make it—or not make it.

If you are in a management position in a company that is seeking to enter the government market, take this advice to heart. Call a couple of these people, tell them who you are and what you do, and get a little advice up front so that you understand the landscape and have a better feel for what *you* need before you enter this market.

I want to end with an article written by Robert Silverman of ReachSolutions (www.ReachSolutions.com) and Steve Charles of ImmixGroup (www.ImmixGroup.com), which is reprinted with permission.

"TEN TIPS FOR TECHNOLOGY MANUFACTURERS IN THE GOVERNMENT MARKET"

Robert Silverman, CEO, ReachSolutions, and Steve Charles, Cofounder and Executive Vice President, Immixgroup

With government spending about to dramatically increase, technology manufacturers are rightly pursuing and making investments in the government marketplace as a strong and stable source of revenue. Dozens of new technology companies enter the government market each year and an even larger number of companies are trying to expand or reenergize their public sector presence now. What are the common themes of those organizations that have found success in this market?

Over the years, working for, and consulting with numerous technology companies selling to the government, we have discovered these tips, primarily because so many entrants fail to achieve the level of success they expected.

1. *Government business strategy clearly defined*

A clearly defined government business strategy is critical for new entrants as well as companies looking to scale to the next level. Without a complete business plan, few companies establish a track record of success and sustained revenue growth year after year. While commercial success and having "cool technology" will always generate a few sales in the government market; these elements alone won't build a sustainable business over the long run.

To drive success and build a scalable business, a government business plan with sufficient breadth and depth is a prerequisite. More than just an overview of the market and a statement of general tactics, a government business strategy identifies the organizational and infrastructure requirements and establishes a clear focus for sales, channel alliance programs, marketing, contracting vehicles and delivery efforts required. Further, the strategy will include an actionable plan and ROI [return on investment] analysis tying revenue forecasts and timelines with resources and investment requirements under various scenarios.

2. *Government market opportunity clearly identified*

The U.S. government is the largest single consumer of commercial technology products in the world. If your company is successfully selling in the commercial sector, there are likely sufficient requirements in the government sector to justify entering the market. The question you need to answer when determining your potential government market opportunity is not whether there is a market for your products and services, but precisely where in the government is your greatest market opportunity.

The most successful technology companies focus carefully on the most relevant targets of opportunity in the company's commercial sweet spot and thus avoid chasing empty envelopes. The same is true in government. Those companies that are disciplined about positioning their products to address specific problems that they are uniquely capable of solving vis-à-vis their competition (not always another manufacturer), gain traction and increase market share by repeating the sales process in government agencies across the entire government sector.

3. *Government treated like a sector, not a vertical*

Only a few commercial technology companies make a concerted effort to understand precisely how the government sector is different from the private sector. This sector spans quite a few verticals like transportation, finance and healthcare. Each agency has a unique mission. Each has its own language, values and rules. Multiple verticals combined with this different culture make entering the government market more like expanding into a foreign region than a new industry.

The government market requires a unique approach to selling, marketing, partnering and contracting. Companies that understand and embrace this uniqueness, while leveraging their commercial processes to keep it simple and streamlined, are the most successful.

4. Synchronized expectations

Setting realistic, attainable revenue expectations, and delivering on that commitment, is what builds the corporate trust for making the investments necessary for year-over-year growth. These expectations need to include both the timing and the amount of revenue forecasted. While it no longer needs to take two to four years to achieve success in the government, this market remains a momentum play, requiring early balance and focus on laying the correct foundation to generate downstream ROI. When developing a government strategy it's critical to define both your revenue and non-revenue milestones.

The revenue forecast and its relationship to the required level of resources and investment, whether internal or external, covering activities ranging from business development, sales, operations, legal, financial, marketing, channels, and contracts need to be established. All too often the government sales staff cobbles together the channel, the contract vehicles and the marketing messaging while corporate looks on passively, not fully understanding, appreciating and supporting the business requirements of the government market. A corporate plan for the government market that defines both revenue and non-revenue milestones and links these to required investments and corporate support will result in shared expectations and focused execution.

5. *Making the right investments*

It's often not a question of whether enough investments are made. More often than not, a company's government initiatives are not part of critically analyzed and focused marketing strategy. This leads to investments being made in the wrong places at the wrong time. Making initial key investments combined with the right resources driven by a well thought out government business strategy can make an order of magnitude difference in results.

6. *Balancing tactical and strategic activities*

Many companies fail to develop sustainable traction in government because they do not balance short-term tactical needs with longer-term strategic requirements. Turning initial traction into sustained market momentum requires a balance between tactical and strategic activities. A government strategy that focuses exclusively on short-term, tactical revenue opportunities does not establish the necessary foundation for longer-term program or enterprise-wide deals. Conversely, government teams that focus on strategic programs at the expense of tactical revenue fail to deliver sufficient results soon enough to justify further investment. The most successful companies establish the right balance between measurable tactical sales and programmatic business development activities necessary to sustain growth.

7. *Identifying and executing a repeatable process*

Quick initial success is sometimes the worst thing that can happen to a technology company unfamiliar with the government market. Companies that, for example, close a sole-source deal or get handed a "bluebird" by a systems integrator begin to assume future deals will be closed just as easily. Expectations are raised and revenue forecasts are increased without doing the hard work of creating a repeatable, predictable business.

There are no silver bullets or short cuts to building a strong business in the government sector. Building a sustainable government business requires companies to implement a repeatable sales process with infrastructure components such as opportunity identification, compliant contract vehicles, service delivery partners and relevant market messaging as part of a coordinated strategy.

8. *Government team support is part of the corporation's plan*

In many cases, government sales initiatives do not get the attention, support, or government-specific resources needed for early success. Because of the unique requirements of the government market, the same corporate resources that created the company's success in the commercial market seldom have the necessary experience in the government market to adequately support the government program. Because the government market is often not well understood by corporate commercial departments, the government team often receives insufficient support forcing the team to fend for itself usually with mixed results. Successful government programs are built upon the strong support and involvement of the entire company.

9. *Sales practices measured*

Technology companies typically find it difficult to evaluate the effectiveness of the business development, sales, marketing and alliance activities necessary in the government sector. Commercial processes and metrics need to be modified to accurately measure the unique activities and drivers of the government market. Viewing the government sales process and pipeline quality as a black box generally leads to false measurements. Don't assume that your government sales team is failing or being successful in the absence of meaningful metrics that realistically measure the business development and sales pipeline.

10. *Prepare to scale*

Government programs often stall because they fail to put in place the organization, processes and investments necessary to evolve to the next stage of their development. Government programs need to progress through multiple stages in order to increase penetration and market share. Depending upon the stage, the program will need to update its organizational structure, practices, support infrastructure, and market approach.

Government programs that continually assess and adapt their strategy, processes and capabilities at each stage with an eye toward evolving to the next one can avoid a Darwinian fate.

In summary, companies can build successful and sustainable government businesses if they understand and appreciate the unique aspects of the government market, they approach the market strategically, and they commit the right resources and investments. Usually this requires investing in talent that has a track record of success in this market.

ABOUT THE AUTHOR

Mark Amtower is a nationally recognized expert on marketing to the government. Since he started Amtower & Company in 1985, he has advised hundreds of companies on both successful entry into the government market and on market share growth once established. His clients have ranged from *Fortune* 100 companies to very small businesses and everything in between. He has been quoted in over 175 publications worldwide and has spoken at over 250 events, including keynote and lunch speeches. He is the author of *Government Marketing Best Practices* (2005) and *Why Epiphanies Never Occur to Couch Potatoes* (2007). His weekly radio show, *Amtower Off Center*, airs Mondays at noon on Federal News Radio in Washington, DC, and is simulcast on www.FederalNewsRadio.com. In 2008, he was recognized by *B2B* magazine as one of the top 100 business marketers in the United States. He is a popular speaker at government and business marketing events, where he is known for his candor and all-black attire.

INDEX

MARK AMTOWER LIVE AT YOUR EVENT!

When your event needs an authority on doing business with the government, look no further! Bring in the "Godfather of Government Marketing"!

Mark Amtower is a frequent speaker at government and industry conferences, trade shows, and company events throughout the United States. He is available for keynote and lunch speeches, half-day and full-day workshops, and seminars.

Amtower is known for his dry wit, candor, and realistic approach to doing business with the government and for his all-black attire. Using stories from his vast experience in the government market, Amtower keeps the attention of his audiences while he educates them on the various nuances of the government market.

Long recognized as one of the best in marketing to the government, Mark Amtower can be a valuable addition to your program.

Visit http://www.federaldirect.net/speaker.html for more information.

Mark Amtower is also available to consult with *your* company.